THE
DIVERSITY
FACTOR

IGNITING
SUPERIOR
ORGANIZATIONAL
PERFORMANCE

JAMES T. MCKIM, JR., PMP, ITIL

The Diversity Factor: Igniting Superior Organizational Performance

Publishing and Design:

EP&C AUTHOR
P U B L I S H I N G

Ordering Information: Quantity sales. Special discounts are available on quantity purchases by corporations, associations, and others.
Contact: info@organizationalignition.com or
visit http://www.organizationalignition.com

First Edition: March 2022

ISBN: 9798809873321

For more information about James McKim or to book him for your next event or media interview, please visit:
http://www.organizationalignition.com

To my wife Nancy in appreciation for allowing me to grow and learn about business and life

Table of Contents

PART 3: Diversity and Organizational Performance

PART 4: Preparing to Ignite Superior Organizational Performance Through Diversity

Introduction

Igniting superior organizational performance can happen through diversity, equity, and inclusion that creates a sense of belonging for every stakeholder of the organization.

Organizations today are faced with ever evolving, ever more demanding and diverse customers. They are faced with doing more with less while still striving to be more efficient in their operations. And they are faced with pressure to be socially conscious.

Diversity is touted as a solution to (or at least a tool in) addressing all three of those challenges. But is diversity really the solution for *your* organization? What are the potential benefits? How can you tell if your organization could benefit from diversity efforts? How do you convince management to dedicate resources to such efforts? How do you make the changes necessary to achieve those benefits?

During 30+ years of experience working in and with small and large organizations in the private and public sector internationally, I have seen first-hand that organizations underperform because of lack of diversity, equity, and inclusion. This book is for any leader in an organization looking for ways to increase organizational performance. Whether you are in senior leadership and constantly asking:

➢ How can product/service packaging/roll-outs go more smoothly?

> ➢ Why are our products/services not getting traction with diverse audience or losing sales to competition?
> ➢ How can I improve customer/client satisfaction?

or you are in HR asking:

> ➢ How can I improve employees trust in each other and in the organization?
> ➢ How can I reduce the attrition that is costing money to hire/train replacements?
> ➢ How can I diversify my workforce?
> ➢ How can I reduce the increasing complaints of discrimination or unwelcoming workplace?

or you are in Operations or Management asking:

> ➢ How can I make my team perform more efficiently or consistently?
> ➢ How can I make sure employees know how to perform their jobs effectively?
> ➢ How do I know if my diversity efforts are successful?

This book is designed to help you answer those questions and improve your organization's:

> ➢ Efficiency (which includes quality)
> ➢ Effectiveness
> ➢ Relevance
> ➢ Financial viability

In this book you will learn how to:

> ➢ Inspire creativity and drive innovation
> ➢ Improve your marketing effectiveness
> ➢ Attract and retain the best talent
> ➢ Offer a broader and more adaptable range of product and services
> ➢ Encourage high-performing teams by onboarding, engaging with, and making diverse people feel valued

> ➤ Provide greater opportunity for personal and professional growth which will reduce attrition; and
> ➤ build trust among diverse people.

Studies by organizations such as Deloitte, McKinsey, PWC (formerly Price Waterhouse Coopers), and the World Economic Council confirmed that diverse organizations outperform their peers who are not diverse by upwards of 80%. But the writings on how to achieve these results seemed to be piecemeal. Books and articles that exist seem to focus on the human side of the equation in an organization. How having a focus on diversity brings out the best employees? How leaders can be inclusive. A scant few focus on the financial benefit of diversity. All good and needed.

But this book goes further. It pulls those pieces together on one place. And it goes beyond the notion that financial benefit is the only business case for diversity to talk about

This book is meant to be a resource. While it provides anecdotes and a roadmap, it is not a substitute for a change management effort led by senior level management in your organization

The experiences shared here are in no way reflective of all possible situations. This book provides a starting point and a guide. The stories and guidance are meant to inspire introspection of your organizational that will lead to positive change.

As you go through this book, think about how the stories and situations compare with where your organization is in its journey to superior organizational performance.

Part 1: Diversity: Good or Bad for your Organization describes what organizational performance is and the reason diversity will ignite superior organizational performance.

Part 2: Definitions explains the definitions of key terms: Diversity, Race, Gender, Age, Neurodiversity, Implicit Bias, White Privilege/Normativeness, Equity, Inclusion, Belonging, culture - the race/ethnicity type.

Part 3: Diversity and Organizational Performance describes how diversity impacts the Organizational Performance system in an organization as described by Curt Howes

Part 4: Preparing for Igniting Superior Organizational Performance Through Diversity defines success through the PWC Maturity Model and describes the levers available to an organization in moving up the maturity model and the Roadmap achieving superior organizational performance which follows the base Plan-Do-Check-Act change management model. It, also, outlines the 5 Magic Guideposts toward change to a more diverse, equitable, and inclusive organization.

Part 5 Beginning the Journey to Igniting Organizational Performance Through Diversity describes what it will take to set the tone for a successful diversity, equity, inclusion (DEI) effort and what types of DEI goals the organization should establish.

Part 6: Igniting Superior Organizational Performance Through Diversity describes the Roadmap to Discovering Organizational Performance steps to design, implement, check, and act/adjust the actions that will achieve the goals established in Part 5.

Are you ready to ignite your organization's performance? Keep reading...

PART 1

Diversity: Good or Bad for Your Organization?

Reasons for Diversity and what diversity looks
like in an organization.

CHAPTER 1

Why Discuss Diversity in an Organization?

"A diverse mix of voices leads to better discussions,
decisions, and outcomes for everyone."
—Sundar Pichai

Thesis: *Diversity is a key to organizational performance.*

 Dr. Robert Livingston, Professor of Psychology at Harvard University, is fond of making the case for diversity by using the analogy of tools in fixing or building a structure. If all you have is a screwdriver, how can you hammer in or pull out a nail? How can you measure the distance between two studs for accuracy? How can you screw a nut onto a bolt? A screwdriver alone will not do. You need a tool belt of diverse tools.

This is a wonderful analogy for why it is important to discuss and have diversity in an organization. There are many jobs that need to be performed in an organization. If all you have in an organization full of people who look, talk, and think alike – for example, all have an expertise in sales - then how you can your organization be good at accounting? Manufacturing? Digital Marketing? Compliance? Customer Service? Sales expertise alone will not do. Those jobs require different talents and skills. You need people with those different talents and skills in order for the organization to perform well.

"Of course it isn't a case of sexual discrimination. We just don't think you're the right man for the job."
CartoonStock.com

SORRY, MY CLIENTS DON'T LIKE THE COLOUR OF YOUR TIE...
PANCHO

"I thought outside the box. Now they won't let me back inside!"
CartoonStock.com

And we need to look at more than just diversity of talents and skills. Imagine three separate cartoons.

1. A woman sitting on the floor in front of a desk behind which sits a White man who is saying, "Sex Discrimination? What are you talking about?"
2. An African-American male sitting in a chair across the desk from a White man who is saying "Sorry, my clients don't like the color of your tie."
3. A White male dressed in a business suit standing outside a what appear to be boardroom doors who comments to a woman passing by, "I thought outside the box. Now they won't let me back inside!"

Each cartoon seems to be depicting different behavior. Sexism in one. Racism in the second. And narrow-mindedness in the third. Yet they all have something in common – an underlying issue. There are obvious issues on the surface, but what is the underlying issue that spans all three of these cartoons? When these cartoons are shown in the workshops I have delivered, and that same question is asked, I hear responses such as these:

➤   power discrimination

- ➢ lack of understanding and awareness of one another
- ➢ denial
- ➢ the perpetrator often does not know that they're being discriminatory
- ➢ the one talking not acknowledging the issue
- ➢ not accepting the difference of the person in front of them.

While these are all issues, there is an underlying issue not being acknowledged. As the responses hint, underlying each is a power dynamic. A dominant person, the person in power, is not valuing the other person for who they are.

In the first panel, the manager is only seeing the individual in terms of gender, not recognizing that he is looking at her on the floor. In the middle panel, the hiring manager is focusing on the color of the Black man's tie, not valuing him for what he has to offer substantively. The third panel is a little different, isn't it? It's not about outward appearance. It's about the way that the person outside the door thinks. His way of thinking/perspective/point of view is why whomever is in power behind the doors is not letting him in.

Overall, what we are really discussing is valuing individuals for who they are and what they bring to the table, rather than how they appear or think. For those in power, this is a missed opportunity to gain insights that can drive innovation, sustainability, relevance, and financial viability.

To put this in organizational terms, these are some questions you may want to ask:

- ➢ Do you want improved organizational performance, or are you happy with your current organizational performance?
- ➢ Do you want to reach a larger or more diverse customer base?
- ➢ Do you want to improve your customer satisfaction rates?
- ➢ Do you want to be more innovative?
- ➢ Are your customers complaining about your product features or service quality being insufficient for their needs?

You have probably heard the phrase *a business is only as successful as its employees,* or something similar. So, let's look at these questions and diversity's impact at the organizational level and the individual employee level,

Diversity at the Organizational Level

My thesis is that diverse organizations that are inclusive and equitable perform better than their peers in many respects. As organizational performance pioneer Edward E. Hubbard says, "Simply put, utilizing diversity as a strategic asset keeps an organization's competitive edge sharp for the long haul."[1] Organizations are more innovative, sustainable, relevant, and have greater financial viability. This section explores these benefits, which are desired by for-profit and nonprofit organizations alike.

Innovation

Renowned economist Joseph Schumpeter defined innovation as "the practical implementation of ideas that result in the introduction of new goods or services or improvement in offering goods or services."[2]

The World Economic Forum's report "Diversity, Equity and Inclusion 4.0: A toolkit for leaders to accelerate social progress in the future of work" states that companies with diverse employees have "Up to 20% higher rate

of innovation and 19% higher innovation revenues."[3] Think of the most innovative companies (e.g., Google and Apple). Each have very diverse employees.

According to another World Economic Forum article, the reasons for organizations to work toward diversity include disruption and innovation as well as sustainability.[4]

The coming together of people of different ethnicities with different experiences in cities and societies is a key driver of innovation. The food that we eat every day is a result of this blending of cultures. The most successful musical genres, such as jazz, rock'n'roll, or hip-hop are the products of cultural amalgamation.

Sustainability

Here, we are discussing the long-term existence of the organization – not the long-term impact on the environment, community, or society as a whole. In a report called "Shaping the Sustainable Organization," Accenture and the World Economic Forum use the definition of creating "lasting value and equitable impact for all stakeholders."[5] We can look at sustainability from two perspectives: internal and external.

Internally, organizations do not exist without people. So, to be sustained, there must always be people willing to work for the organization over the long-haul. But how is that achieved?

Utilizing a workforce sustainability perspective, the World Economic Forum describes a "Millennial Quotient." By the year 2025, 75% of the global workforce will be made up of millennials - which means this group will occupy the majority of leadership roles over the coming decade. They will be responsible for making important decisions that affect workplace cultures and people's lives.[6]

This group has a unique perspective on diversity. While older generations tend to view diversity through the lenses of race, demographics, equality and representation, millennials see diversity as a melding of varying experiences, different backgrounds, and individual perspectives. They view the ideal workplace as a supportive environment that gives space to varying perspectives on a given issue.

The 2021 Deloitte Millennial Survey shows that 74% of these individuals believe their organization is more innovative when it has a culture of inclusion.[7] If businesses are looking to hire and sustain a millennial workforce, diversity must be a key part of the company culture. The survey also shows that 47% of millennials are actively looking for diversity and inclusion when sizing up potential employers. Companies will stay relevant only if they have a diversified employee base going forward.

Another article states that "Age diversity has proven to improve That leads to greater sustainability."[8]

Aura Huot, Director of People and Culture at Lavallee Brensinger Architects, commented:

> "In today's market, if people don't care about anything else they need to care about the retention of the workforce as it is extremely expensive. And most organizations have no idea of the actual costs of cost of losing one employee a year. Never mind [the cost of] finding them. That has an impact [on] not only the financial, but also the culture of the organization."

Externally, organizations are influenced by what society is, does, or thinks. What counts for good employment practices in society dictate what will attract and retain employees. The 2020 census reveals some interesting trends with respect to diversity:

- ➢ unprecedented stagnation in population growth;
- ➢ a continued decrease in Americans' geographical mobility;
- ➢ more pronounced population aging;
- ➢ a first-time decline in the size of the white population and rising racial and ethnic diversity among millennials, Gen Z, and younger groups (which now comprise a majority of the nation's residents);
- ➢ the crucial role immigration will play in future population growth.[9]

In sum, this seems to point to a more diverse society. And as the population becomes more diverse, societal norms become more diverse. Thus, in order to keep employees, an organization needs to know the trends and understand those societal shifts around the employee base and build a culture that is welcoming to as many people in that employee base as possible. Otherwise, it will suffer attrition, not be able to attract new employees, and eventually be forced to fold.

Not only is it important to understand societal norms from an employee perspective, it is also important to understand societal norms from the perspective of the perception of the organization, and its reputation– at the most basic level of how society sees organizations. In Northwestern Nat Life Ins. Co. v. Riggs (203 U.S. 243 (1906)), the Supreme Court accepted that corporations are, for legal purposes, "persons." This means that corporations (organizations) separately from their associated human beings (e.g., owners, managers, or employees), have at least some of the legal rights and responsibilities enjoyed by natural persons. They have a right to enter into contracts with other parties and to sue or be sued in court in the same way as natural persons or unincorporated associations of persons.

In reality, organizations are very different from individuals. Individuals do not produce products or services that require many people to produce or have an impact on a larger number of persons. An organization's reputation is tied to the product and services it produces and the way it behaves in the communities in which it has its presence. If an organization behaves in ways that are perceived as going against societal norms or expectations—say, being discriminatory toward a demographic or a member of a demographic that society believes is worthy of being treated fairly—then the organization will lose not only sales or clients but also the ability to retain and attract new employees over the long term.

An example of how discriminatory actions have implications for an organization's reputation is fast-food restaurant Chick-fil-A. Despite Chairman Dan Cathy's statements against same-sex marriage, the company's generous funding of anti-gay groups, and the claims that the outspokenly Christian corporation doesn't discriminate against workers, the company has been sued at least a dozen times for employment discrimination.[10] This has caused minorities across the country to boycott the restaurant and bring its sustainability into question.

As you may have been sensing, sustainability feeds organizational relevance, so let's discuss that.

Relevance

Organizations exist to serve some purpose. They provide products or services for individuals (i.e., business-to-consumer, or B2C) or other organizations (i.e., business-to-business, or B2B) to consume. Those products and services need to be relevant or they will not be purchased.

One definition of relevance "is the full experience of a product, brand, or cause that we can relate to; it's an experience that not only changes minds, but, importantly, changes behavior–and sustains that change."[11]

Thomas Baekdal—founder of Baekdal Strategies, media analyst, author, and publisher—does an excellent job of visually describing relevance as the intersection of one's concern, one's internets, and the usefulness of a product or service.[12]

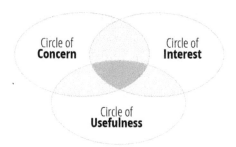

Exhibit 1.1 Circle of Relevance

From a marketing perspective, multicultural campaigns have a higher ROI than their non-diverse counterparts—as much as 40% higher, according to a study by Nielsen as reported in the Baekdal article![13] For example, Coca-Cola found multicultural marketing reaps greater return on marketing investment (ROMI)[14] Multicultural marketing would not be possible with without a diverse workforce.

Sarah Judd Welch, Principal & CEO of Sharehold, says that DEI is important for your customers and clients. "…clients don't talk about DEI during initial conversations but when they do research into the company, DEI comes up."

Attorney Nick Holmes, with the law firm Devine Millimet, shared that a national construction firm has a special emphasis on DEI because it needs more workers. The firm recognizes that folks with Confederate flags on the back of pickup trucks aren't attractive to diverse workers.

Denise Lamoreau at Atos shared this with me:

> "Obviously, employees are looking to work for companies that have a purpose of value back to the communities, meaning to the work they do. And our work in the decarbonisation space has really lent itself to that type of person, which is to our advantage, but you know, we have to make sure we're marketing ourselves correctly to reach those people."

VP of HR Brie Elliott at Ballentine Partners indicated they are looking to have an impact on the financial industry by working with the Certified Financial Planning board to support four to five scholarships per year.

From a competitive advantage standpoint, as Nannan Hu, founder and former executive at Greenhouse Software, says, "I think a big competitive differentiator for our organization was the organizational diversity and commitment to D&I that we had."

This relevance is a major component of Financial Viability.

Financial Viability

Aura Huot from Brensinger Architects makes the point that by delaying DEI, you are delaying organization profitability and legacy.

McKinsey has tracked DEI for years: it looked at more than 1,000 companies in 12 countries, measuring not only their profitability (in terms of earnings before interest and taxes, or EBIT) but also longer-term value creation (or economic profit). McKinsey found the top-quartile financial performing corporations that embrace gender diversity on their executive teams were more competitive and 21% more likely to experience above-average profitability. They also had a 27% likelihood of outperforming their peers on longer-term value creation. Different perspectives on customer needs, product improvements, and company wellbeing fuel a better business. Organizations that embrace diversity in ethnicity are 33% more likely to be more profitable than their peers.[15]

In addition to organizations paying attention to DEI because of how it influences internal performance, diversity is so important to the bottom line of organizations that companies build their businesses around it. Nannan said:

> "We were very much in the diversity and inclusion space: we actually had a module in our software that helped organizations improve in that particular area. So, we had a product that helped companies...highlight unconscious biases... And while biases are not always bad, because they help us make faster decisions in daily activities, when it comes to hiring, it's not so good, right. ...So, our goal was to help organizations realize that DE&I was not just something that you should do so that you feel good about yourself, that you feel like a decent human being. But at the end

of the day, that it actually has positive bottom-line benefits for your company or your organization. And... when you're talking to C-level folks...that's really what they care the most about."

For much more detail on how diversity impact financial viability, I suggest you read *The Diversity Scorecard: Evaluating the Impact of Diversity on Organizational Performance* by Edward E. Hubbard.

Diversity at the Individual Employee Level

At the individual level, DEI fosters belonging, which motivates peak performance. One study showed that a strong sense of employee belonging leads to a 56% increase in job performance, a 50% drop in turnover risk, and a 75% reduction in sick days.[16] For an organization of 10,000 employees, this translates to a savings of $52 million. (Later, we will discuss how to achieve this employee sense of belonging.)

As Aura Huot shared with me, "... when a person is saying that more people and more people and more people are leaving ... at [the] individual level, it makes you question your place in the organization. And it makes you question why those people leave, (was it) because they found better jobs? That's what you hope. Or if they left because something was done to them." We know that an individual's identity is tied up with their job. So, a person questioning their connection with the organization (which results in decreased performance) is real.

Aura also observes that, in business, we like to say what happens to you at work is not personal. But "At the end of the day, the people that work in organization are individuals, and it's personal, right? You come to work to do an effort, and the team becomes part of your community."

Key reader takeaways

This chapter started with the thesis that diversity is a key to organizational performance. Throughout the chapter, we saw stories and research highlighting why diversity is important to address in an organization from the perspectives of innovation, sustainability, relevance, and financial viability. It is also important to address diversity for individuals, as research proves they are more likely to remain with an organization and be more productive if the environment is one that includes diversity and equity.

➢ Innovation is achieved from new/unique ideas. More new/unique ideas come through engagement and inclusion of people with diverse backgrounds and experiences.

➢ Sustainability (organizational) is achieved by retaining high-performing employees over a long period of time. Having employees for a long period of time comes from creating an organizational culture and environment where diverse people want to be. We pay special attention to attracting and retaining younger people because of the Millennial Quotient and the fact that Millennials will live longer and run our organizations in the long run.

➢ An organization's reputation is shaped by society and shapes how people react to it.

➢ Relevance is achieved by giving clients and customers what they want. A larger customer/client base means a more diverse customer/client base. A diverse employee base allows for the understanding of what that diverse customer/client base wants, and how they want it.

➢ Financial Viability is achieved through the combination of innovation, sustainability, and relevance, which makes an organization more competitive and more profitable.

Consider This...

This chapter explored why diversity is important for an organization.

➢ What is your motivation for exploring diversity, equity, and inclusion?

➢ What is your current rate of innovation?

➢ How sustainable is your organization?

➢ How financially viable is your organization?

Creating a diverse workforce where everyone feels they belong and can perform at their best is no small feat. It takes a commitment to change. This kind of change can take months if not years to accomplish. Here are some questions you should ask yourself to see if you are ready to make this commitment:

Question	Your Response
Are you willing to be comfortable in uncomfortable situations?	
Are you willing to commit to identifying the time and resources to achieve organizational performance even when it may not seem to bring short-term gain?	
Are you ready to learn how to get the actual backing of your organization's Board and leadership, not just lip-service?	

If you answered "yes" to these questions, then you are ready to move to the next step toward benefiting from diversity. One must recognize this as a Change Management effort in an organization. Successful change begins with a vision of what things should look like. Thus, the next chapter explores what diversity in an organization looks like.

CHAPTER 2

What Does Diversity Look Like?

"Diversity is being invited to the party; inclusion is being asked to dance."

—Vernā Myers

Thesis: *There are many signs that indicate whether an organization has been successful in engaging diversity in beneficial ways.*

Diversity is about more than just having diverse people. As Vernā Myers says, diversity is being invited to the party. But having a diverse work force alone is not sufficient to achieve organizational performance. That diversity must be included in all areas of an organization, or as Myers puts it, "asked to dance." I would add that even those two alone are not sufficient to achieve superior organizational performance. The third ingredient is equity. Being asked to dance like everyone else does not take advantage of an employee's unique gifts. To allow people to blossom, they have to be asked to dance the way they want to dance. This is why we are really talking about diversity, equity, and inclusion (DEI).

But, how do we know what diversity, the DEI kind, really is? As with anything we try to achieve, it is important to understand what success looks like. As a student of philosophy, I know that in addition to understanding what something is, it can be instructive to understand what something is not.

In this case, we are discussing how an organization achieves superior performance through diversity. So, this chapter begins with a grounding in demographics before exploring what diversity looks like from a macro level (organizations in society) and a micro-level (within an individual organization) in terms of characteristics and behavior and employee perceptions.

Current Demographics

As we go through this thought process considering what diversity looks like for an organization, it is helpful to keep in mind the demographics of the population.

Race

Visual Capitalist" https://www.visualcapitalist.com/visualizing-u-s-population-by-race/ shows the current makeup of the United States by race. Trends from the same source show that by 2060, the United States will be a minority-majority country, with people of color outnumbering people socialized as White.

Age

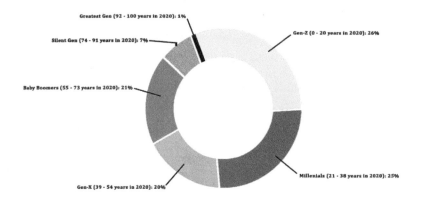

Total US Population by Generation in 2020
Share of total population

Exhibit 2.1 Total US Population by generation in 2020

The current makeup of the United States by age as shown in Exhibit 2.1 Total US Population by generation in 2020 is:

- ➢ 1% Greatest Generation
- ➢ 21% Boomers
- ➢ 20% Gen X
- ➢ 25%Millennials
- ➢ 26% Gen Z

The Urban Institute "What the Future Holds" article (https://www.urban. org/policy-centers/cross-center-initiatives/program-retirement-policy/ projects/data-warehouse/what-future-holds/us-population-aging shows) Exhibit 2.2 shows the trend that the U.S. population is aging.

Number of Older Americans, 1960-2040 (in millions)

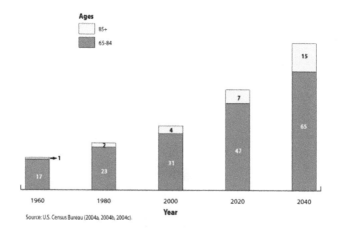

Source: U.S. Census Bureau (2004a, 2004b, 2004c).

Exhibit 2.2. The U.S. Population Is Aging

Gender

Exhibit 2.3 shows the current makeup of the United States by age and gender.

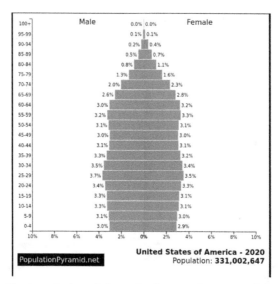

Exhibit 2.3. The Population of the United States, in Terms of Gender and Age
Source: Population Pyramid:
https://www.populationpyramid.net/united-states-of-america/2020/

Although the gender percentages have stayed fairly constant over time, more people of both sexes are identifying as LGBTQ+, as shown in Exhibit 2.4.[17]

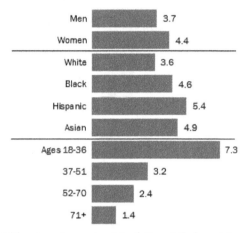

Exhibit 2.4. Older Americans Are Much Less Likely to Identify as LGBT

Furthermore, fewer younger Americans say they are attracted only to the opposite sex when compared to older cohorts, as shown in Exhibit 2.5.[18]

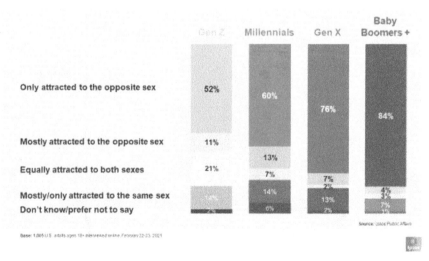

Exhibit 2.5. Sex Attraction of Different Age Groups in the United States

Disability

The CDC reports that 22% of adults have some sort of disability.[19] Exhibit 2.6 elaborates.

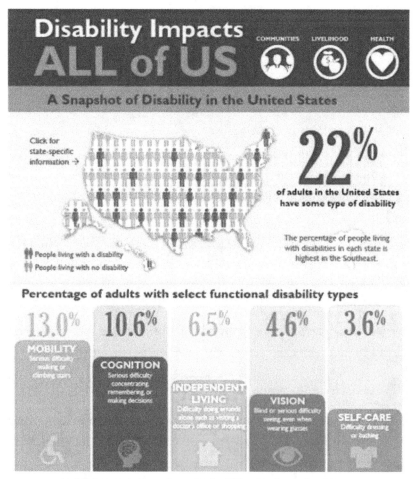

Exhibit 2.6. A Snapshot of Disability in the United States

Socioeconomics

The Urban Institute reports population by income class, as shown in Exhibit 2.7.[20] The report states that the trend is that the population in the upper middle class and the rich is growing while the population of poor and near poor remains relatively consistent.

Growth of the Upper Middle Class

Share of U.S. population in each income class. The biggest change since 1979 has been the 16 percentage point increase in upper middle-class families.

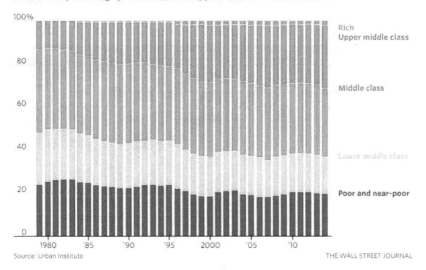

Source: Urban Institute   THE WALL STREET JOURNAL

Exhibit 2.7 Growth of the Upper Middle Class in the United States, from 1980

Macro Level

As we look at organizations as a group in society, we see some interesting statistics about their characteristics, behavior, and impact on society.

Characteristics & Behaviors

According to McKinsey, diverse workers are not evenly spread across all sectors or positions. And they are not equitably compensated. [21] The McKinsey report makes the following points.

First, Black workers are concentrated in lower-paying service industries. The report notes: "Frontline workers were deemed essential at the height of the Covid-19 pandemic and helped ensure Americans stayed fed, clothed, and cared for medically. that large shares of Black workers in these industries earn less than $30,000 annually."[22]

Wall Street has recognized it has a major issue with lack of racial diversity. For example, Citigroup published a report entitled "Closing the Racial

Inequality Gaps" that made the case that "Not addressing racial gaps between blacks and whites has cost the U.S. economy up to $16 trillion over the past 20 years.... If these racial gaps were closed today, we could see $5 trillion of additional GDP over the next 5 years."[23]

Another McKinsey study points out five common challenges that materially affect Black representation, advancement, and experience:

➢ Entry-level jobs are a revolving door, and Black employee attrition is high.
➢ Black employees encounter a broken rung from entry-level jobs to managerial jobs.
➢ A trust deficit exists between Black employees and their companies.
➢ Black employees lack the sponsorship and allyship to support their advancement.
➢ Frontline jobs largely do not connect Black employees with sufficient opportunities to advance.[24]

Second, the McKinsey report also indicates that women are not well-represented in the corporate ladder. The McKinsey report states:

"Women have made gains in corporate America but they remain underrepresented. Today, women still make up less than 25% of executive-level positions. And now, burnout from the pandemic has forced even more women to leave the workforce altogether."

Also, AARP reports that older workers are being discriminated against, as shown in Exhibit 2.8.[25]

A Pew Research describes the inequality of income and wealth continuing to increase for the upper class and decreasing for the middle class as shown in Exhibit 2.9.[26]

Exhibit 2.8. Discrimination Against Older Workers

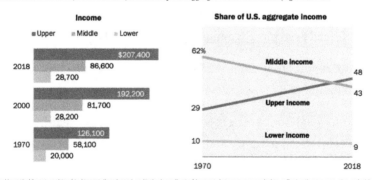

Exhibit 2.9 Upper-Income, Middle-income, and Lower-Income Inequities

Employee Perceptions

Where there is a lack of diversity, equity, and inclusion caused by bias, employees do not feel they can bring their authentic selves to work. And there is a cost to the organization. When asked about the cost of bias, Sylvia Ann Hewlett, an economist and the founding president and CEO of the Center for Talent Innovation, said this:

> "It's only natural that when employees feel the burn of bias, they downsize their contributions at work—accumulating to a hard hit on company bottom lines. Employees at large companies who perceive bias are nearly three times as likely (20% vs. 7%) to be disengaged at work. That kind of clock-punching is costly. Gallup estimates that active disengagement costs U.S. companies $450 billion to $550 billion per year."[27]

Micro Level

As we look inside organizations, we see some interesting statistics about their characteristics and behavior.

Characteristics and Behaviors

Having executives who are inclusive is one sign of diversity in an organization. Armando Llorente, noted DEI Consultant, shares the story of an executive team that made a determination that diversity and inclusion would be a critical element of the business—just as important as profitability, quality, and other factors. Members of the senior leadership team were all assigned responsibilities as sponsors, or champions, for various affinity groups that were set up within the organization.

When the company reported to Wall Street on a quarterly basis about what was happening from an overall profitability or acquisition (or some other business beat), there was also an update with regards to human resources. The report included what was happening not only from an overall staffing perspective, but also along the lines of what the company was doing in terms of training hours dedicated to attention to diversity and inclusion. Topics ranged from the time that new hires came into the business and were familiarized with the strategy, the philosophy of the organization, and their actual assignment in a particular group or division within the company.

In Armando's story, the management team took an active role in making DEI happen by sponsoring affinity groups and attending their meetings. It signaled that senior leadership was committed to achieving performance through diversity.

Some other signs that an organization is leveraging diversity are:

➢ Employee satisfaction is high.
➢ Ideas are flowing from everyone in the organization.
➢ Customer satisfaction is high.
➢ The average tenure of employees is high.
➢ Sales are greater than your competitors.

On the flip side, what are some ways that a lack of diversity manifests at the organizational and individual employee levels? Exhibit 2.10 lists a few of these.

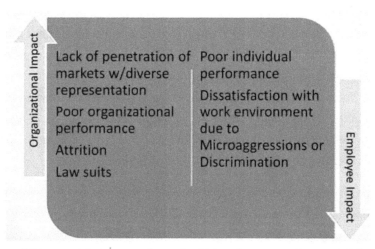

Exhibit 2.10. The Impact of a Lack of Diversity on Employees and the Organization as a Whole

Organizational Perspective

"When there is a misalignment in mission and actual operations, [lack of] DEI is frequently the cause," Sarah Judd Welch, CEO of Sharehold shared with me.

In many cases, we see organizations that are not really looking at diversity, equity, and inclusion and don't have the market penetration that they could have—and probably should have. They have poor organizational performance. There is attrition in your organization because people don't feel valued. We all want to be valued as individuals. If an employee is not feeling valued, that employee is going to leave. As Edward Hubbard noted, "Employees will often cast their vote of dissatisfaction and level of commitment by using the Law of Two Feet (i.e., they go somewhere else)." This is why we have the "Great Resignation" of workers now: they are not feeling valued. Janine Skinner from Atos described to me the lack of DEI as "Some I have interviewed indicated they have been talked over or not listened to at meetings."

Employees are burned out. They're not being rewarded for the extra hard work that they're putting in, especially during this time of a pandemic. Colleen Clark, Head of HR at Life is Good, shared with me that when she started at the company, lack of DEI manifested as disparities in salaries.

Lack of DEI can appear as a double-standard being applied to white people vs. people of color.

In a conversation I had with Nannan Hu he observed, "...when minorities get assertive, they're seen as aggressive right? And when white people are assertive, they're seen as seen as like, a positive thing, right?" Also, he has seen that Asian Americans are often seen as workers rather than leaders. For example, we see this manifest as getting passed up for promotions white folks being taken aback by a vocal/assertive Asian-American like him."

Also, a lack of DEI can lead to lawsuits. Think about it. If someone is discriminated against in an organization, there is potential for lawsuits. In the United States, laws about equal treatment of employees are monitored by the Equal Employment Opportunity Commission (EEOC rules). Attorney Walter Foster of Eckert Seamans shares the story of the Chicago Blackhawks who had a video of a coach sexually assault a woman just before the playoffs. It was reported, but the leaders did not do anything until three weeks later because they were afraid it would derail the team's playoff chances. Unfortunately, he states that discrimination cases are a growing area for his firm.

To see what organizations are taking the lead in diversity, take a look at the *Forbes* article "2021 America's Best Employers for Diversity."[28]

Employee Perspective

All of the above helps us to think about DEI from an organizational performance perspective. And there are many more impacts than we could list here. But what is the impact of not having a DEI lens from an individual's perspective? What does it look like?

A Pew Research Center survey of LGBT adults showed that 92% of its respondents said that "compared with ten years ago, society is now more accepting of people who are LGBT." Yet the same Pew survey found that more than one in five LGBT employees have experienced some form of workplace discrimination.[29]

As I and others have said, employees don't want to perform for an organization that doesn't value them. So, they will perform poorly because they are dissatisfied with their work environment. This happens when they experience microaggressions often or trauma from a significant discriminatory incident.

Noted Economist Sylvia Ann Hewlett commented about retention and innovation:

> "Those who perceive bias are more than three times as likely (31% to 10%) to say that they're planning to leave their current jobs within the year.... Finally, bias appears to sap innovation. Those

who perceive bias are 2.6 times more likely (34% to 13%) to say that they've withheld ideas and market solutions over the previous six months."[30]

Key reader takeaways

Looking at diversity is really looking at the equitable inclusion of diverse people. Demographic trends indicate that the workforce is becoming more and more diverse in terms of race, ethnicity, by age, ability, and socioeconomics. However, there is much inequity in how people are treated.

At a macro (i.e., societal) level, diversity looks like industries where regardless of their group—race, age, gender, disability, and socioeconomic status—pay is equal. The ratio of the number of employees from various groups in various positions in organizations is on par with the number of people from those groups in society

At a micro (i.e., organizational) level, diversity looks like high employee and customer satisfaction and ideas flowing from everywhere in the organization.

Consider This...

This chapter explored what diversity looks like.

- ➢ What are the demographics of your organization?
- ➢ How do those demographics compare with the area or customer base you serve?
- ➢ What is your attrition rate?
- ➢ From whom in your organization do most ideas come?
- ➢ Do you perform at least an annual employee survey to know how your employees feel?

With a vision of what diversity (equity, and inclusion) look like, the next step is to understand some key definitions. Some questions you should ask yourself to see if you are ready to move to this next stage in your journey are in the table below.

Question	Your Response
Are you ready to be part of an organization where you may not be in the majority?	
Are you ready to learn about and embrace definitions of terms that may be different than what you thought they meant?	
Are you ready to commit to creating win-win situations between your organization and its employees?	

If you answered "yes" to these questions, then you are ready to move to the next step toward benefiting from diversity: coming to a common understanding of terms that we tend to throw around without stopping to think about what they really mean. Thus, the next chapter explores definitions of such terms as organizational performance, diversity, equity, inclusion, race, gender, ethnicity, and age.

PART 2

Definitions

Definitions of key terms related to diversity, equity, and inclusion as well as organizational performance.

CHAPTER 3

What Is Organizational Performance?

"How can you govern a country which has 246 varieties of cheese?"

—Charles de Gaulle

Thesis: *Organizational Performance is about more than just the financial bottom line.*

Organizational
Performance
• Effectiveness
• Efficiency
• Relevance
• Financial Viability

Exhibit 3.1 IOA Organizational Performance Model

Leaders look at organizations in terms of organizational performance, which can be defined in terms of a framework referred to as the Institutional and Organizational Assessment Model (IOA). It was created by Universalia and the International development Resource Center. This framework is more fully elaborated in the book Organisational Assessment: A Framework for Improving Performance by Lusthaus et al. "The framework defines an organization as a good performer when it balances effectiveness, efficiency, and relevance while being financially viable." So, let's look at each of these aspects one by one.

Effectiveness

Effectiveness has to do with how well an organization fulfills its mission. It speaks to the impact an organization actually has. The effectiveness of an organization can be described in terms of how well the organization performs the following.

- ➤ **Executes its major programs:** For example, achieves outcomes such as levels of increased literacy, miles of new roads, percent of girls obtaining education, new employment, level of research productivity, level of community health—areas directly linked to an organization's mission and function.
- ➤ **Meets client expectations:** That is, how well groups inside the organization meet expectations: how well an organization meets the expectations of its external customers or clients in terms of quality of services or products.
- ➤ **Meets functional responsibilities:** For example, if the mission of the organization is about education (coverage, student achievement), how well is it fulfilling that mission.
- ➤ **Provides useful services:** For example, how well services are delivered to clients or beneficiaries; how well technology is transferred to those who purchase it from the organization.

Exhibit 3.2. Efficiency Through Inputs to Outputs

The Academy to Innovative HR (AIHR) Digital uses Exhibit 3.2 and defines organizational effectiveness as:

"...the degree to which an organization achieves the goals it set out to achieve. These goals can be a certain output (productivity or service quality), efficiency goals it set out for, but also the degree to which its internal processes are aligned, and the degree to which it has secured the resources required to create a competitive advantage."[31]

If you have done any work with processes before, you know (as shown in Exhibit 3.2) that there is an input to a process, and there's an output from that process. The output is where productivity comes in. The resources are the inputs, the outputs are whatever it is that you're trying to produce.

Efficiency

Efficiency has to do with getting the most out of resources available in fulfilling the organization's mission. efficiency is success in producing as much output as possible from available input. The efficiency of an organization can be described in terms of:

> ➤ Cost of products and services—benchmarked comparisons, if possible
> ➤ Cost of providing internal managerial services—benchmarked comparisons
> ➤ Perception of efficiency of key work procedures and flows
> ➤ Stretching the financial allocations
> ➤ Staff productivity (turnover, absenteeism, research outputs)

Exhibit 3.3 is a proposed model of organizational efficiency: the authors of the article in which this appeared state that organizational efficiency is "the relationship between inputs and outputs of a given activity." This is similar to the description of effectiveness some people use. I maintain that looking at the relationship between inputs and outputs is really a measure of efficiency.

As the article states, "Diversity management and teamwork (tm) are significant predictors of organizational efficiency. They positively influence organizational efficiency because organizational harmony and teamwork, which are fallouts of diversity management, stimulate organization's competence in finding strategies to produce at cheaper and better ways and better allocation of resources."

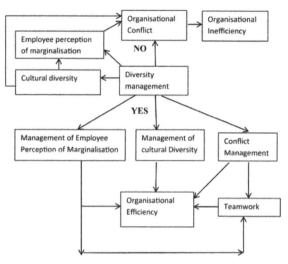

Exhibit 3.3. Organizational Efficiency Flow

Source: "Managing Diversity for Organizational Efficiency" by <u>Inegbedion</u>, <u>Eze Sunday</u>, <u>Abiola Asaleye</u>, et. al.
(<u>https://doi.org/10.1177%2F2158244019900173</u>)

Relevance

Relevance has to do with whether clients and customers find programs, products, or services address their needs or wants over time. Relevance can be viewed in terms of:

> ➤ Adaptation of mission and products/services to meet stakeholders' needs
> ➤ Adaptation of operations to the ever-changing environment
> ➤ Maintenance of a good reputation
> ➤ Sustainability over time
> ➤ Entrepreneurship

There are two parts to relevance: *product/service relevance* and *organizational relevance*.

Product/Service or *brand relevance* is described by Andrea Colville in her book *Relevance: The Power to Change Minds and Behavior and Stay Ahead of the Competition*.

The other type of relevance is *organizational relevance*. This has to do with how the internal workings of the organization are perceived.

Vijay Eswaran, Executive Chairman of the QI Group of Companies, describes that relevant organizations excel at disruption and innovation.32 They also create environments where people want to work. Sound familiar? Chapter 2 described the Great Attrition going on because many organizations do not prove to their employees that they are truly valued.

Financial Viability

Financial viability has to do with profitability and having reliable funding sources. Financial viability comes from good financial planning addressing the components of a financial model, as in Exhibit 3.5, which shows the components of a comprehensive organization financial model.

Exhibit 3.5. Financial Planning Factors

Source: "Simple Financial Planning Models: A First Look," Sumaira Sultana Talpur, Head of Group Accounting & Financial Reporting at Abdulla Ali Bin Haider Group (https://www.linkedin.com/pulse/simple-financial-planning-models-first-look-one-cma-usa-mba-finance/

So, as we think about this notion of financial viability in organizational performance, we ask the questions:

➤ Is the organization financially viable?
➤ Does the organization have multiple sources of funding?
➤ Are funding sources reliable over time?
➤ Is funding linked to growth or changes occurring in the industry or marketplace?

Key reader takeaways

Many people think organizational performance is only about profit. But organizational performance can be defined as a balance of effectiveness, efficiency, and relevance while being financially viable. In short:

➤ Effectiveness has to do with how well an organization fulfills its mission;
➤ Efficiency has to do with getting the most out of resources available in fulfilling the organization's mission;
➤ Relevance has to do with whether clients and customers find programs, products, or services address their needs or wants over time;
➤ Financial viability has to do with profitability and having reliable funding sources driving good financial planning addressing all the components of a financial model.

Consider This...

This chapter explored what organizational performance is.

➤ How effective is your organization in achieving its mission?

➤ How efficient is your organization in achieving its mission?

➤ How relevant is your organization's mission, products, and/or services?

➤ How financially viable is your organization?

This chapter defined organizational performance. Its definition is critical to understand as, in the end, that is what we are trying to achieve.

Here are some questions you should ask yourself to see if you are ready to make this commitment:

Question	Your Response
Do you understand that organizational performance is more than just profit?	
Are you willing to commit to think about organizational performance as more than just profit?	
Are you willing to be open to definitions of terms that may run counter to what you have been taught or learned previously?	

If you answered "yes" to these questions, then you are ready to move on to the next chapter, which defines foundational terms related to diversity but are critical to understand as we seek to achieve organizational performance through diversity.

CHAPTER 4

What Is This Term "Diversity"?

"It contributes greatly towards a man's moral and intellectual health, to be brought into habits of companionship with individuals unlike himself, who care little for his pursuits, and whose sphere and abilities he must go out of himself to appreciate."

—Nathaniel Hawthorne

Thesis: *Diversity is about more than just race or gender. It is really about equitable inclusion of diverse people so that they feel they belong, bringing their authentic selves to work.*

Exhibit 4.1 Diversity Word Cloud

Ask people what the term "diversity" means, and you will likely hear many different answers. The word cloud (aka wordle) shown in Exhibit 4.1 appears in many places on the Internet and includes words people identified when they thought of the word "diversity."

Interestingly, diversity seems to be defined differently by Millennials and Boomers/Gen-Xers as shown in Exhibit 4.2:

> "There is a growing generational gap in how diversity and inclusion is defined in today's workplaces. Millennials, who will comprise nearly 75% of the workforce by 2025, believe inclusion is the support for a collaborative environment that values open participation from individuals with different ideas and perspectives and the unique factors that contribute to their personalities and behaviors, which is in stark contrast to prior generations who traditionally consider it from the perspectives of representation and assimilation."[33]

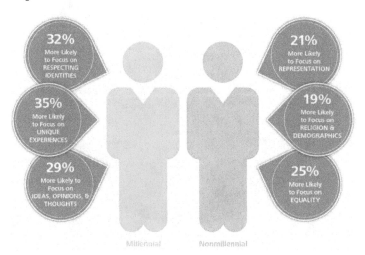

Exhibit 4.2. Generational Perspectives on Diversity

Let's get to defining the concepts surrounding the terms that are key to how we interact in the world: this chapter focuses on these terms:

- ➢ Diversity
- ➢ Ethnicity/Culture
- ➢ Race
- ➢ Gender

- ➤ Age
- ➤ Morality, Ethics, and Politics
- ➤ Inclusion
- ➤ Neurodiversity
- ➤ Equity

Diversity

Here is a textual definition of diversity:

"Differences within and between groups of people that contribute to variations in habits, practices, beliefs and/or values... Diversity includes all the ways in which people differ, and it encompasses all the different characteristics that make one individual or group different from another."[34]

Exhibit 4.3. Diversity Wheel[35]

A "Diversity Wheel" was created to help people understand how group-based differences (attributes) contribute to people's social identities (personality) and to identify the differences that are important in shaping identities particularly the differences that are prone to stereotypes, those that may lead to frustration, suspicion, and conflict when they are not understood or acknowledged.

We each have attributes or characteristics that make up our personality. And that's the focus of diversity. Diversity is our characteristics, what makes us up.

Exhibit 4.3 is an updated version of that original Diversity Wheel.[36] Instead of the terms *attributes* or *characteristics*, Gardenswartz and Rowe use the term *dimensions*. The point here is that there are internal, external, and organizational dimensions of our personality.

Internal (aka Primary) Dimensions

The wheel describes Internal (aka primary) dimensions as powerful/ sustaining differences, having a life-long impact.

For example, we are born on the same day (age), that doesn't change. Yes, our age changes as we get older, but the day that we were born doesn't change.

Gender is discussed in much more detail later in this chapter, but for now, suffice it to say our gender is not likely or easy to change over our lifetimes. Yes, it can change because of advances in science and cultural acceptance. But in general, our gender does not change. Our sexual orientation doesn't generally change over a lifetime.

Our physical ability does not generally change over a lifetime. Yes, we can be injured and, therefore, have less ability. Or we can gain more skills. But physical ability is not something that dramatically changes over our lifetimes, at least not intentionally.

Our race and ethnicity do not change or lifetimes. Although some people of color are melanin-deficient enough that they can "pass" for being White, the physical characteristic of skin color or preferences derived from being of a certain ethnic heritage are lifelong.

Just think, who do you know with these dimensions?

External (aka Secondary) Dimensions

External (aka Secondary) dimensions are other important differences acquired later, potentially less influential, mutable differences.

Our educational background changes, primarily earlier in life when we go through school. Many attain knowledge and skills from attending high school. Fewer attain knowledge and skills from attending a secondary institution. Fewer still attain knowledge and skills from attending a graduate program. Even fewer attain more knowledge and skills from post-graduate work. Others gain on-the-job knowledge and skills.

Most of us strive to make more money than we currently make so that we could have a better lifestyle. Job tenure in 2018 was 4.2 years.[37] These job moves also translate to changes in work experience. They also translate to our geographic location being mutable. We all live somewhere and may work somewhere.

We are not born married. Marriage is about making a formal commitment to another person for life. *USA Today* reports that nationwide, nearly half (48.2%) of all Americans age 15 and over are married.[38]

We are born inquisitive and curious. The military is about command and control. You do what you were told, no questions asked. Anyone who has had military experience can tell you that way of living is not something they were born with and that they had to adjust to it over time.

We are not born knowing much about the world. Religion and ways of thinking are rules we follow as we relate to the world. We learn over our lifetimes how to relate to the world.

Just think, who do you know with these dimensions?

Organizational Dimensions

Organizational dimensions have to do with how we interact in organizations. What's our function in the organization? Are we part of sales, are we part of marketing, are we part of business development?

What is our seniority in the organization? How are we relating to other people in the organization? Are we a senior person? Are we a junior person? Are we management? Are we individual contributors?

Just think, who do you know with these dimensions?

Of special interest to most people are the dimensions of race, ethnicity/culture, gender, age, neurodiversity. So, let's look at these in more detail...

Race

According to the Merriam-Webster dictionary, *race* is any one of the groups that humans are often divided into based on physical traits regarded as common among people of shared ancestry. The key component of that definition is "based on physical traits."

Yet researchers have determined that race is really a "social construct". For example, take a look at this video from VOX: "The myth of race, debunked in 3 minutes" (https://www.youtube.com/watch?v=VnfKgffCZ7U).

There is no "race" gene or chromosome. A recent press release from the American Medical Association states this in no uncertain terms.[39]

While Charles Darwin may have been wrong when he claimed that race was based on physiology, he was onto something. Dr. Dorothy Roberts, a social justice advocate and law professor at the University of Pennsylvania, shares that race is better thought of as a way to group people with certain traits. For definitions of more terms related to race, I recommend reading the glossary of terms related to race from the Racial Equity Tools site https://www.racialequitytools.org/resources/fundamentals/resource-list

There is a saying that we are what we eat and a product of our environment. People in different geographic regions eat certain foods and are exposed to certain environmental factors. Those shape how we look and who we are.

Thus, race is more about family geographic origin and experiences than skin color. That leads us to a discussion of ethnicity and culture.

Ethnicity/Culture

Ethnicity or culture is frequently mixed with race. But ethnicity and culture are very different from race. Where race is about skin color, ethnicity/culture is

Exhibit 4.4. Culture Wheel

"How our bodies retain and re-enact history through the foods we eat; the stories we tell; the things that hold meaning for us; the images that move us."[40]

To be more precise, ethnicity and culture are slightly different concepts. But I see them as different sides of the same coin. Culture is about social behavior, whereas ethnicity is belonging to a group of people who have a certain culture.

Source: https://medium.com/@beautehealthy/what-is-culture-types-of-culture-elements-of-culture-characteristics-of-culture-7b4d65caddc7

The previous section discussed the "Diversity Wheel." This section discusses the "Culture Wheel," shown in Exhibit 4.4. The wheel shows the "elements" of ethnicity/culture; key among these elements are:

- ➢ Values and knowledge which make up beliefs;
- ➢ Traditions & rituals which make up customs;
- ➢ Attitude toward others and society as a whole (i.e., communal eastern ethos vs. individualistic western ethos).

Value Differences

Culture Plus Consulting has a great description of the cultural value differences you need to know as you interact with people:

> "Cultural values are shared ideas of what is good, right, and desirable in a society. They are a Cultures society's preferences for managing external adaptation and internal integration challenges that threaten its survival. Cultural values sit on a continuum between two contrasting approaches to a societal problem. Every culture sits somewhere between the opposing alternatives."[41]

Those alternatives include:

1. Individualism vs. Collectivism
2. Power Distance
3. Uncertainty Avoidance
4. Orientation to Time
5. Gender Egalitarianism
6. Assertiveness
7. Being (less developed world) vs. Doing (more developed world)
8. Humane Orientation
9. Indulgence (less religious/devout) vs. Restraint (more religious/ devout)

Culture/Ethnicity Examples

So now you're probably asking, what are some cultures? Listing cultures is no simple matter. Cultures can be thought of in different categories, such as these:[42]

Western	Eastern
➢ Anglo-American	➢ Indosphere
➢ Latin American	➢ Sinosphere
➢ English-speaking	➢ Islamic culture
➢ African-American	➢ Arab culture
	➢ Tibetan culture

Categories of cultures are shown in the table above and are listed by ethnicity or ethnic sphere. These cross the political divisions (nations, states, etc.) of the world which number over 400 and produce variations of the ethnic cultures listed. Here are the top 10 general cultures in the U.S. according to the medium.com article:

➢ Italian	➢ French
➢ Spanish	➢ Chinese
➢ American	➢ Indian
➢ UK	➢ Greek
➢ Mexican	➢ Swedish

It is important to note that there are differences between even these cultures based on geography. And remember, you can't tell someone's culture just by looking at them.

Do you know someone in any of the top 10 general cultures? What are some of the cultural differences?

To make matters more complex, Dr. Christian Jarrett points to research that indicates different nationalities and cultures really have different personalities. But they are not the same as the stereotypes we hold.[43]

Now that we've seen differences in values with some examples, let's look at some actual cultural differences. According to the English Student Blog (http://www.theenglishstudent.com/blog/understanding-different-cultures), for example, some of the differences in a few cultures include the differences in how to accept gifts, how to greet someone, and how to eat.

Understanding that one culture is not any better than another and being open to embracing that culture is referred to as having *cultural humility*. Knowing how to interact with people from different cultures is referred to as *cultural competence*. We need both to successfully interact and benefit from the diversity around us.

There are so many differences and variations in culture, you may be asking yourself, *how can I deal with the large number of cultures?* For that, you may want to take advantage of a "Cultural Navigator" such as is available here: https://www.culturalnavigator.com.

The next time you see someone do something that you do not think you would do, ask yourself, is this person behaving that way because of their culture?

Gender

When most people think of gender, they think of male vs. female stereotypes. Quick, name some of those stereotypes. Exhibit 4.6 lists one author's identification of gender stereotypes.

Shannon Ann Mitchell in a paper reports stereotypes about males and females are shown in the table below.

Male	Female
Dominant	Submissive
Independent	Dependent
Intelligent	Unintelligent
Rational	Emotional
Assertive	Receptive
Analytical	Intuitive
Strong	Weak
Brave	Timid
Ambition	Content
Active	Passive
Competitive	Cooperative
Insensitive	Sensitive

Of course, those stereotypes are not always true.

In actuality, gender has several components as described by a paper by students at Coastal Carolina University, https://scalar.usc.edu/works/ index-2/media/the-gender-spectrum originally at calar.usc.edu/works/ index-2/media/the-gender-spectrum.

Those components are as follows.

> **Sex:** referring to the biological anatomy of an individual. A person can be totally biologically male, totally biologically female, or have biological features of both.

> **Gender identity:** referring to how someone sees themselves. They can see themselves as a man/boy, as a woman/girl, or somewhere in between referred to as" transgender," "genderqueer," or (as Indigenous peoples have known for quite some time) "two-spirited."

> **Gender expression:** referring to how all someone wants to be seen—e.g., male and wants to be seen as being masculine, feminine, or androgynous (i.e., neither or both).

> **Sexual orientation:** referring to gender to whom they are attracted. Either only to women, only to men, to both, or to none.

Who do you know that does not fit the stereotypical male or female?

Age

Quick, what are some characteristics of people from different generations? Some would say old people can use technology. Others would say young people are impatient. If others would say that all people are too stuck in their ways.

Exhibit 4.5 from the Human Resources Exchange Network, shows the different generations of people currently in the workforce. It describes the influences, values, work preferences and styles, and career needs for each of those generations.[44]

	Traditionalists	Boomers	Gen X	Millennials
Born	1922-1943	1943-1960	1960-1980	1980-2000
Influences	Great Depression; military model; formality; patriotism; atomic bomb	Korean War; Civil, Women and Reproductive Rights and Ecology Movements; Woodstuck, Sputnik; TV; dual incomes	moon landing; Watergate; MTV; video games; ATMs; CNN; Web; latchkey; divorce	9/11; Challenger; cell phones; pagers; computers; IM
Values	respect; security; loyalty; obedience	challenge; ambition; achievement; power	leadership; freedom; truth; independence	safety; loyalty; security; hope
Work Preferences and Style	hierarchical command and control; formal environment with dress code and strict conduct rules; one job, one employer	politically savvy; competitive environment; challenge authority for feedback; opportunity seekers; frequent job changers	work-life balance; skeptical of authority; self-reliant; oppose hierarchy; innovative; intentional, frequent job changing	diverse culture; collaborate; meaningful work; fun at work; flexibility
Meeting Career Needs	define and build legacy; annual feedback outlining contributions	define promotional opportunities; annual feedback on progress with documentation	define career path expectations; real time feedback on progress	define career path opportunities; real time feedback on progress and alignment

Exhibit 4.5. Characteristics of Different Generations

I would note that there does seem to be some dispute as to the date as to the last year when Boomers were born and the first year when Gen-Xers were born. I have seen some of presentations where the last boomers were born in 1964. But I would submit that none of these dates are hard and fast. For example, my parents were born in 1917 and 1921—i.e., before the traditionalists. However, when I was growing up, I could tell that they were definitely influenced by the Great Depression as they always stocked up on anything they could for fear that they did not know what to turn the economy would take.

There is one generation missing from Exhibit 4.8. Can you guess what generation that is? Gen-Z. What is interesting to note is that members of Gen-Z do not know a world without the Internet.

Neurodiversity

In addition to differences in physical characteristics, there are differences in the way people think. The term *neurodiversity* was coined by Executive Function Coach/Education Coach Seth Perler to refer to how different brains learn differently. I think it is valuable to understand the concepts of thinking styles and the notion of morality, ethics, and politics (discussed later in this chapter).

Thinking Styles & Brain Dominance

There is evidence that we each exhibit different thinking styles. From brain dominance to neurodivergent thinking, there are many ways people think.

Ned Hermann developed the Hermann Brain Dominance Instrument (HBDI) Whole Brain Thinking Styles to describe ways that people think.[45] See Exhibit 4.9.

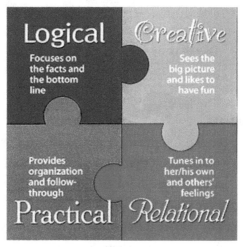

Exhibit 4.6. Whole Brain Thinking Styles

There is a wonderful joke to illustrate the different thinking styles. Consider a person who is inside a tunnel. As shown in Exhibit 4.6, we can think in one of the following ways:

- ➢ Pessimist (Logical) who sees a dark tunnel and fears there is no way out;
- ➢ Optimist (Creative) who sees a light at the end of the tunnel;
- ➢ Relational (Sensitive) who feels the cool temperature of the tunnel;
- ➢ Realist (Practical) who sees a freight train coming and tries to figure out how to not be killed.

The punchline for the joke is that the Train driver sees 3 idiots standing on the tracks.

Lest you think, I don't always think in one of the styles, Hermann says we are all capable of each of these styles, but we also have a "go-to style"—a style we slide into when we are stressed or short on time. To illustrate the impact of this, consider two people in a heated argument. The person trying to make a point gravitates to a *logical* thinking style. She is spouting off facts and figures to make her case. But the other person gravitates to a *relational* thinking style. So, he only takes in the way that the other person feels based on the emotion he is sensing from her. The facts and figures go in one ear and out of the other. This is one reason why conversations can be difficult.

There are other thinking style and behavioral models similar to the Hermann Whole Brain Thinking Model. There is the DISC model and the infamous Myers Briggs model. It is not important to know all of them or to choose one over the other. What is important is to learn about the people around you, however, so you can know how to better interact with them.

Neurodivergence

Another aspect of neurodiversity is the notion of neurodivergent ways of thinking—that is, having a brain that functions in ways that diverge significantly from the dominant societal standards of normal. Dr. Rick Walker, Professor of Psychology at California Institute of Integral Studies, coined this term.[46]

Examples of neurodivergence are ADHD, Turrets Syndrome, Dyslexia. Dr. Walker posits that what we think of as is neurological diseases are merely different ways that brains process information. We all have our strengths and weaknesses.

People who are neurodivergent should not be looked at as sick, but as having special gifts and needing help and some areas. None of us really is exactly the same in our processing capabilities. We all have our strengths and we all need help in certain areas.

For example, one young man was diagnosed with ADHD when he was a teenager. He could hyper focus and make fantastic presentations with Microsoft PowerPoint. But he had difficulty turning in his homework on time. He now has a highly-responsible job at a pharmaceutical company. Clearly, he is making significant, positive contributions to society with his neurodivergent brain.

Morality, Ethics, and Politics

If you thought the previous sections on race and gender were a bit bold as I delved into subjects not usually discussed in conversations around organizations, hold on to your hats. I'm going even deeper into the taboo subjects of value systems which lead us to the topics of morality, ethics, and politics. More colloquially, who's right and who's wrong?

As noted in the section on culture, people have different value systems. Their value systems provide a lens through which they interpret ideas and information. These value systems are described as *morals*, which refer to an individual's own principles regarding right and wrong, and *ethics*, which refer to rules provided by an external source—such as codes of conduct in workplaces or principles in religions. These play out in our lives, as we interact in groups, as *politics*.

Of course, our personal value systems shape how we interact and make decisions. For a much better understanding of this, I point to Jonathan Haidt's book, _The Righteous Mind: How Good People Are Divided by Politics and Religion_. The two theories he describes, which I think are most important to think about from an organizational perspective, are Jeremy Benthem's "Dimensions of Cognitive Style" (which Haidt describes on pp. 137) and his own Moral Foundation Theory (which he describes starting on pp. 141).

Benthem's dimensions, shown in Exhibit 4.7, describes the relationship between someone's level of empathy and his or her level of desire for systemization or efficiency.

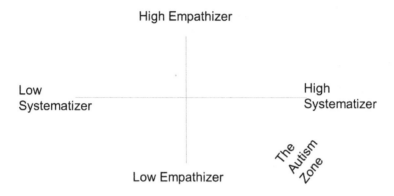

High Empathizer

Low Systematizer

High Systematizer

Low Empathizer

The Autism Zone

Exhibit 4.7. Benthem's Dimensions of Cognitive Style

This model allows us to understand someone's behavior if we know them well enough:

Systematizers are always looking to improve the system.

Empathizers are always looking to improve how people feel.

For example, someone who is a high systematizer and low on empathy would rank high on the autism scale. Leaders such as Steve Jobs come to mind here, as an example of a leader who high on systematization and low on empathy. He got things done, but the tone he set for the workplace was not very inviting.

Haight's own Moral Foundation Theory is shown in Exhibit 4.8. It indicates that morality depends upon six factors, or what he called *tastes*, which are shown across the top.

	Care/ Harm	Fairness/ Cheating	Loyalty/ Betrayal	Authority/ Subversion	Sanctity/ Degradation	Liberty/ Oppression
Conservative	X	X	X	X	X	X
Liberal	X					(X)

Exhibit 4.8. Haidt's 6 Tastes

He further describes that conservatives and liberals have different tastes. It is not that both conservatives and liberals don't have the same taste, but that conservatives seem to put an equal value on all tastes, whereas liberals seem to place a higher value on the tastes of care/harm and liberty/oppression.

Think about the people you know who are conservatives of liberals. Do they fit this model?

Now that we've defined dimensions of personality value systems, you may be asking yourself, *how do they impact an organization?* Let's move on to the concepts of equality, and equity.

Equity

What would you say is the difference between *equality* and *equity*? Between equal treatment and equitable treatment? Exhibit 4.9 helps us to see the difference.

| In the first image, it is assumed that everyone will benefit from the same supports. They are being treated equally. | In the second image, individuals are given different supports to make it possible for them to have equal access to the game. They are being treated equitably. | In the third image, all three can see the game without any supports or accommodations because the cause of the inequity was addressed. The systemic barrier has been removed. |

Exhibit 4.9. Equality Vs. Equity

Now, what is interesting is to think about the third panel in Exhibit 4.8, where no youth is given any boxes to stand on, but they still are able to see the game. So, there's a slightly different word that can be used to describe that third panel. "Equity" is a word that that some people would use for that. But for me, the third panel goes beyond the equitable treatment. Some people have described it as inclusiveness - removing barriers? Some people use the word "justice." Some people have used the word "liberation."

What I find very interesting about this third panel is that if you think about it, that third panel is actually cheaper for the ball park than the other two. Why? I say that because I look at what is *not* in that panel. The boards are not in that panel. The ballpark didn't have to spend the money to purchase boards, and it doesn't have to spend money to maintain the boards.

In one of my workshops, someone asked, Isn't the fence a barrier? *why couldn't the ballpark get rid of the fence altogether?* My response was, jokingly, that I think the ballpark would call it pandemonium. But all kidding aside, the fence is there for safety. So, I would not call it a barrier.

I encourage you to think about this in terms of the world and your own organization. In some cases, there are barriers that are being put up in front of people that are actually costing us all. The costs of equipment and/or the people who have to maintain those barriers.

What barriers in your organization can you remove so that everyone has an equal opportunity to achieve their goals?

Inclusion

Exhibit 4.10. Inclusion Word cloud

If I were to ask you what words come to mind when you think about "inclusion," what words would you use? Exhibit 4.10 is a word cloud that was created when a group was asked for words that represent inclusion. One word that I think is interesting that's not here is *welcome*. *Partnership* is another word I am surprised is not there.

For those of you who are learn or comprehend better through text, here's a definition from the American Association of American Colleges and Universities.

> "The active, intentional, and ongoing engagement with diversity in ways that increase awareness, content knowledge, cognitive sophistication, and empathic understanding of the complex ways individuals interact within systems and institutions. The act of creating involvement, environments and empowerment in which any individual or group can be and feel welcomed, respected, supported, and valued to fully participate."

There are four words that I want to make sure to highlight here: *active, intentional, ongoing,* and, *engagement.* Inclusion is more than just providing equal access. To use a grammar analogy, inclusion is a verb. An intentional action – engagement - with a direct object of people, not an environment that is equally acceptable. And for someone to feel like they are included, this action must be ongoing – not merely a one-time transaction.

To reiterate, diversity is not inclusion. Inclusion is intentionally engaging with diversity in the form of diverse people.

Now on to Belonging...

Belonging

If I were to ask you what it feels like when you belong, what would you say? What are the characteristics of the group or environment where you feel like you belong?

Research says that belonging involves both mental and physical wellbeing. A feeling of emotional safety. A feeling of physical safety. Here's how one researcher describes five primary characteristics of belonging:

> ➤ Where I have a role or responsibility;
> ➤ Where people look like me;
> ➤ Where I am valued and cared for;
> ➤ Where my racial identity and culture is recognized and valued; and
> ➤ Where I share interests or values with others [47]

Employees and members of organizations rank organizations by whether they feel they belong.

I invite you to think about if you feel you belong in your organization and what role diversity, equity, and inclusion have in that feeling?

Key reader takeaways

The term *diversity* is frequently defined by employing more Black people and/or more women. What we should really use as the definition of diversity is people with diverse dimensions. Life-long dimensions such as race, age, or gender, etc. or malleable dimensions such as experiences, ways of interacting with the world such as income, geography, thinking styles, etc.

Initiatives to create a welcoming/inclusive organization are referred to as Diversity, Equity, and Inclusion (DEI) initiatives. Sometimes, "Belonging" is added to the name of the effort to make the acronym used "DEIB". Sometimes "Justice" is added to make it Justice, Equity, Diversity, and Inclusion (JEDI). This is because having a diverse workforce itself is not sufficient to create welcoming/inclusive/high-performing organizations.

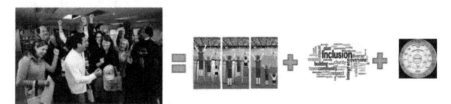

Exhibit 4.11. Formula for Welcoming/Inclusive/High-Performing Organizations/Societies

My formula for organizational success that puts together these definitions is as follows - *"Welcoming/Inclusive/High-Performing organizations/societies exhibit equitable (not just equal) inclusion of diverse people (aka DEI)"*

Consider This...

This chapter encourages us to think about our individual personalities and the personalities of our organizations.

From an individual perspective, consider these questions:

- ➢ When and how did you first become aware that there was such a thing as racial/ethnicity differences, and that people were treated differently on the basis of those differences?
- ➢ Growing up, what contact did you have with people whose racial and ethnic heritage was different from your own? What kind of guidance or models did you have for relationships with those people?
- ➢ Answer the same questions about your early experiences around gender, physical ability, religion, and politics.

➤ What are some foods you eat that are family favorites? Why are they favorites?

From an organizational perspective, consider the questions:

➤ What is the racial breakdown of your organization?
➤ What is the gender breakdown of your organization?
➤ What is the age breakdown of your organization?
➤ What is the physical ability breakdown of your organization?
➤ Do you know where people in your organization fall in the table of Moral Foundation Theory?

This chapter defined diversity and the fundamental concepts necessary to have a language with which to have conversations around organizational performance through diversity. Here are some questions you should ask yourself to see if you are ready to use this knowledge:

Question	Your Response
Do you understand that diversity is about more than just race or gender?	
Are you willing to commit to seeing different experiences and backgrounds as a strength to be leveraged by your organization?	
Are you willing to interact positively with help from others to understand the many facets of diversity?	

If you answered "yes" to these questions, then you are ready to move on to the next chapter, which explores the cause of the lack of equitable inclusion of diverse people in the pursuit of being a high-performing organization.

CHAPTER 5

What Is the Cause of Lack of DEI?

"Somebody who only reads newspapers and at best books of contemporary authors looks to me like an extremely near-sighted person who scorns eyeglasses. He is completely dependent on the prejudices and fashions of his times, since he never gets to see or hear anything else."
—Albert Einstein

Thesis: *Implicit Bias is the root cause of not achieving DEI&B manifesting itself through White Privilege/Normativeness in organizations.*

Organizations are made of people. Thus, the existence or lack of DEI&B is because of people. If we are going to change the way we and people in our organization interact with others, we need to understand the reason, the root cause of why we interact the way we do.

How we see and interact with people is biological as well as learned through socialization. This chapter explores the root cause of social behavior toward those not like us, implicit. It does so by exploring our biological proclivity to bias; how the Cycle of Socialization cultivates and exacerbates implicit bias; and the manifestations of implicit bias that are the cause of our resistance to DEI as individuals.

Implicit Bias: The Root Cause

Brain parts (Triune Brain model)

Neocortex (Human brain)
- The newest, most advanced
- Rational thinking
- A new brain
- Higher level of thinking
- Language, imagination, ideas

Limbic system (Mammal brain)
- Emotions, feelings, dreams
- Habit control
- Memories
- Interaction with others

Reptilian Brain
- The instinctive brain
- Basic body functions
- Unconscious

Amygdala (Lizard brain)
- The oldest part of the brain
- Survival Brain
- Fs (Food, fight Flight)
- Alarm
- Fear, pleasure, anxiety, anger

Exhibit 5.1. The Triune Brain Model

Neuroscience tells us that we are wired to be biased. Paul D. MacLean proposed the Triune Brain model, shown in Exhibit 5.2, which suggests that the brain is divided into 3 parts: reptile, mammal, and human.

1. The "Reptilian Complex" (as MacLean called it) consists of the "reptilian" and "lizard" parts of the brain. They are the oldest and act as the "survival" part of the brain. All of our senses feed billions of bits of data into the reptilian part every second through the brain stem. The data is processed immediately by the amygdala or lizard part. This is our food, fight or flight, and sexual instincts part of the brain. It also rules over much of our other "higher-nature" sections of the brain. This may be why humans have such a hard time evolving into peaceful beings.

2. The "Mammalian brain" is responsible for much of our emotions, memories and habits. It controls many of our quick decisions.

3. The "Human brain" (neo cortex) is what separates us from animals and gives us the ability to understand our world in an incredible

fashion. It gives us language, consciousness, imagination, creativity, reasoning, and many other amazing abilities.

Unfortunately, when the very strong reptilian brain takes control, the neo cortex (human brain) is nearly powerless. When we see anything (animal, vegetable, or mineral) different from ourselves, our amygdala immediately sends cortisol through our bodies in preparation to fight, flee, or freeze. The mammalian part of our brain immediately generates emotions of anger, hatred, fear, and stress based on the data being processed by the amygdala.

This happens in milliseconds without us thinking out it. (If we did have to think about it, we might be killed by that tiger in front of us.) Thus, the term "amygdala hijacking" (lizard brain) has been created to help us understand what happens to us. This is Implicit Bias.

Those are the mechanics. But what is the processing that is going on?

Our brains need to make sense quickly of those billions of bits coming into our amygdala. Our brains do that by using a mental model called the "Ladder of Inference," shown on the left in Exhibit 5.2.

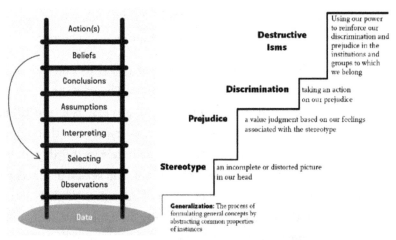

Exhibit 5.2. Ladder of Inference & Steps toward "isms"

Source: Chris Argyris and Peter Senge, *The Fifth Discipline: The Art and Practice of the Learning Organization,* graphic from https://www.toolshero.com/decision-making/ladder-of-inference/

The model shown in Exhibit 5.2 describes our perception of the world, starting from senses to the series of mental steps that need to be taken to work towards an action:

1. **Observations:** We start at the bottom with the data pool that comes in through our senses.
2. **Selecting:** We select facts to pay attention to, based on our values, beliefs, and prior experiences.
3. **Interpreting**: We interpret those facts giving them a personal meeting.
4. **Assumptions:** We make assumptions about what we are observing based on the meaning we have given those facts.
5. **Conclusions:** We draw conclusions based on values and beliefs, and prior experiences.
6. **Beliefs:** We confirm or form new beliefs based on our conclusions.
7. **Actions:** We take action based on our beliefs about how to act on those conclusions.

To describe this process in terms of how we see a person, we use the Steps to "Isms" on the right of Exhibit 5.2:

1. **Generalization**: We select (selection) properties of a person to pay attention to and generalize the data about them (observations) abstracting common properties of that person. For example, "this person looks like someone I've seen somewhere before."
2. **Stereotype:** We then create a picture in our head of what this person's personality is – based on those we know who look like this person (interpreting). Note we don't really know this person so we have no way of knowing if the stereotype fits.
3. **Prejudice:** We then make a value judgment (assumptions, conclusions, beliefs) of whether this is a good or bad person based on our feelings associated with the stereotype. "Brains evaluate everything in terms of potential threat or benefits to the self, and then adjust behavior to get more of that good stuff and left of the bad."[48] For example, all of us are bombarded with the notion that

black males are dangerous, so that is what we believe. Thus, the quick conclusion is that the black male in front of us is dangerous.[49]

4. **Discrimination:** We then decide what action (or actions) to take based on our prejudice (experience and beliefs about what action should be taken around people like this).

5. **"ism":** When there is a power dynamic involved and we have power over the person with whom we are interacting, then we are taking part in an *ism*. If the other person is of a different race, then it is *racism*. If the other person is of a different sex, then it is *sexism*. If the other person is of a different age, then it is *ageism*. In fact, the same behavior interacting with anyone with any of the dimensions from the diversity wheel can be classified as an *ism*.

We are bombarded by so much information that our brains automatically filter. Some of the information we filter out is actually useful and important and might cause us not to rely on implicit bias to determine how we act. This raises the question, "When does implicit bias hijack our brains and our behavior?"

Exhibit 5.3 summarizes this.

Information Overload

Feelings Over Facts

Need for Speed

Emotional/ Cognitive Depletion

Exhibit 5.3. Conditions for Implicit Bias Hijacking the Brain

Bias kicks in when we are in situations where the following conditions occur:[50]

➢ **Information overload**: When there is too much information, ambiguous evidence, or many factors to consider in making a decision.

> **Feelings over facts/Emotional Overload:** When we have strong feelings about something, we tend to be driven by our beliefs rather than by facts. Our impulses and beliefs can override our logic and thinking processes.

> **Need for speed/Fear of Threat:** We take shortcuts to act quickly. Often, these time-savers are based on bias and can be simplistic, self-centered, and even counterproductive.

Emotional or cognitive resources are depleted: when you're hungry/low on sugar.

Cycle of Socialization

While we are not born biased with respect to people different than ourselves, or knowing about the concepts of diversity, equity, inclusion, or belonging. However, "studies from the '90s and early 2000s show that infants categorize people by race at three to six months old. These studies found that infants gazed longer at new faces of people who were the same race as their primary caregiver than at those of a different race, so this is how we know that they're nonverbally recognizing and categorizing based on race."[51] That's right: we know about differences between people and begin to have preference of who we see as good or bad as early as three to six months old.

How we see and learn how to interact with people can be described as a Cycle of Socialization. Identified by Bobbie Harro, 1997. The cycle helps us understand the way in which we are socialized to play certain roles, how we are affected by issues of oppression, and how we help maintain an oppressive system based upon power. We look at lives through three lenses:

1. Lens of Identity: We are born with no lens to view the world but ourselves.
2. Lens of Socializing & Teaching: We are socialized and taught about the world.

3. Lens of Experience: We live and see how others live which gives us experience with the world.

Once we have an understanding of the world, we have a choice. We can take no action to change it - which perpetuates the cycle of how people learn and are treated. Or we can take action to change the *status quo*.

And so, this socialization can be viewed at multiple levels. The Cycle comprises three arrows, three circles, and a core center. Each of these components represents the following:

1. The beginning of the cycle, depicted by the first circle, represents the situation into which we were born. We have no control over this. We are also born without bias, assumptions, or questions. We are either "lucky" to be born into a privileged situation or "unlucky" to born into an underprivileged situation.

2. The first arrow represents that fact that our socialization process begins immediately. We are given a pink blanket if we are a girl or a blue one if we are boy. The rules and norms are already in place and we subtly (and in many cases not so subtly) are made aware of the rewards of conforming and the consequences of rebelling.

3. The second circle represents the institutions that help shape our views and beliefs, and help instill within us prejudice or acceptance.

4. The second arrow represents the way in which the instilling of ideas, beliefs, and behaviors reinforce the cycle of oppression. Behaving differently is not as simply as most of us think. We are rewarded for good behavior – conforming to the norms and standards. By the same token, we are punished for bad behavior – questioning or rebelling against oppressive societal norms.

5. The third circle represents the devastating result upon all of us that this self-perpetuated cycle of oppression produces.

6. The final arrow represents a point at which we all arrive – the results of the cycle. We are forced to make a decision, even if that decision is to do nothing. Doing nothing is the easier choice,

especially for those who benefit from the perpetuation of the cycle: we are all victims of the cycle and we are all hurt by it. Oppression hurts the oppressed and the oppressor.

7. And finally, it is the wheel that turns or enables any cycle. At the center or core of the cycle of socialization are fear, misunderstanding, insecurity, confusion, etc.[52]

Manifestations of Implicit Bias

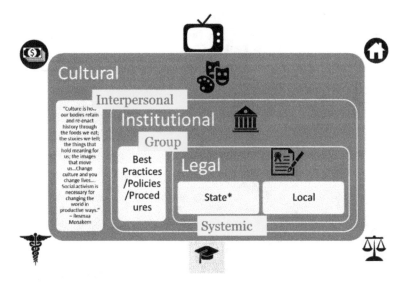

Exhibit 5.4. Levels of Manifestation of Implicit Bias

Now that we understand what implicit bias is and why we all have it, how do we see its impact in ourselves and our colleagues?

Implicit bias manifests at different levels as shown in Exhibit 5.4 Levels of Manifestation of Implicit Bias:

➢ Interpersonal
➢ Group/Systemic
➢ Structural

Let's look at each of these. Exhibit 5.5 provides an overview; the next sections discuss each of these levels in more detail.

Interpersonal Bias

Interpersonal (aka – interpersonally mediated – internalized) can be described as an individual acting in a discriminatory manner. According to a Deloitte 2019 State of Inclusion Survey: 61% experienced bias in their workplaces at least once per month. 83% categorized the biases experienced as indirect or subtle (microaggressions).[53]

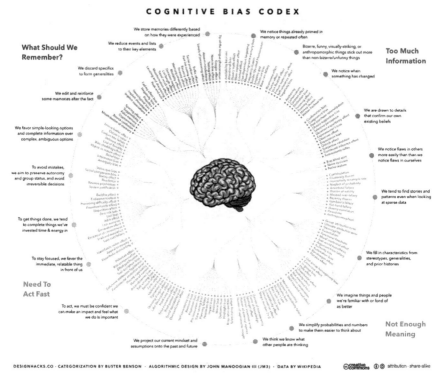

Exhibit 5.5 Cognitive Bias Codex: A Visual of 180+ Cognitive Biases.

Source: https://www.teachthought.com/critical-thinking/the-cognitive-bias-codex-a-visual-of-180-cognitive-biases/

The Cognitive Bias Codex, shown in Exhibit 5.5, maps several of the 400+ known biases when they might occur. As shown in Exhibit 5.6 Types of Biases, there are three types of biases.

Exhibit 5.6. Types of Bias

I like the way Gerd Gigerenzer, director emeritus of the Center for Adaptive Behavior and Cognition (ABC) at the Max Planck Institute for Human Development, looks at implicit bias. He sees them not as errors in judgment, but rational deviations from logical thought.

There are 3 types of biases. Here are some examples of each:[54]

1. Decision-making biases:

➢ *Automation bias:* The tendency to depend excessively on automated systems which can lead to erroneous automated information overriding correct decisions.

➢ *Dunning–Kruger effect*

➢ *Bias blind spot*: The tendency to see oneself as less biased than other people, or to be able to identify more cognitive biases in others than in oneself.

➢ *Zero-sum bias*: A bias whereby a situation is incorrectly perceived to be like a zero-sum game (i.e., one person gains at the expense of another).

2. Social biases:

➢ *Group Attribution error*: The biased belief that the characteristics of an individual group member are reflective of the group as a whole or the tendency to assume that group decision outcomes reflect the preferences of group members, even when information is available that clearly suggests otherwise.

- ➤ *In-group or Affinity bias:* The unconscious tendency to get along with others who are like us. It is easy to socialize and spend time with others who are not different.
- ➤ *Puritanical bias*: The tendency to attribute cause of an undesirable outcome or wrongdoing by an individual to a moral deficiency or lack of self-control, rather than taking into account the impact of broader societal determinants.

3. Memory biases:

- ➤ *Consistency:* Incorrectly remembering one's past attitudes and behavior as resembling present attitudes and behavior.
- ➤ *Cross-race effect:* The tendency for people of one race to have difficulty identifying members of a race other than their own.
- ➤ *Stereotypical*: Memory distorted towards stereotypes (e.g., racial or gender).

Emotional Responses

Digging a bit deeper into the emotional aspects of what causes the lack of DEI, we are emotional creatures, whether we want to believe it or not. Consider this:

> "Plato believed that reason could and should be the master; Jefferson believed that the two processes were equal partners (head and heart) ruling a divided empire; Hume believed that reason was (and was only fit to be) the servant of the passions...Hume was right."[55]

Our mammalian brain sees to that.

How we react to people from different backgrounds is influenced by many factors. What are some of those factors?

- ➤ Our own personal experiences with people from that background.
- ➤ What we've heard about people from this background from our families, peers, the media, popular culture, school, religious

institutions, and so on. As an example, think about what we are taught in school. This is what creates what I have heard Dr. Jennifer Harvey call the "fog" of racism. Jacqueline Haessly also describes this extremely well when she discusses the limiting message found in children's textbooks, the media, and business.[56]

➢ Whether we see ourselves as sharing any values, goals, and ways of doing things with people of this background.

➢ Whether people from this background have any control over the things that make them different from us.

➢ How much power we believe people of this background have in our society and any laws or special programs we know about that affect how people of this background are treated.

What causes these reactions?

Ignorance

In this context, ignorance is a lack of understanding that no one person is any better than another, a lack of understanding that everyone has value even if they have different dimensions that you.

Shawn O'Leary at Dartmouth Hitchcock Hospital shared with me that "one of the biggest hurdles to DEI is elitism. It permeates the medical community. This means it is easy to dismiss someone who doesn't have a pedigree."

Greed

Greed in this context is the desire to obtain what Thandeka calls "wages for whiteness" (in her book *Learning to Be White*, p. 77) – what W.E.B. Du Bois refers to as the "benefits of being white in America" (in his book *Black Reconstruction in America: 1860-1880)* Du Bois summarizes these benefits as:

➢ public deference and titles of courtesy;

➢ access to public functions, public parks, and the best schools;

➢ jobs as policemen;

➢ the right to sit on juries;

- ➤ voting rights;
- ➤ flattery from newspapers while other news was "almost utterly ignored except in crime and ridicule."

Thandika goes on to say, "during the late 1800s, for example, practically all white southern men went armed and the South reached the extraordinary distinction of being the only modernized civil country where human beings were publicly burned alive." I believe this explains a lot about the gun rights movement and the propensity of southerners to want to carry arms. But that's a topic for another book.

This "wages of whiteness" served as a kind of workers' compensation—a consolation prize for those who were not wealthy so they would not be counted as losers because they were, at least, White. This belief, however, leads to inefficient and improper use and distribution of wealth and resources, as so aptly described by Robert Reich in his book *Aftershock: The Next Economy and America's Future:* "I will argue here that our fundamentals are profoundly skewed, that the great recession was but the latest and largest of growth of an increasingly distorted distribution of income." He added that "We will have to choose, inevitably, between deepening this consent (and its ever-nastier politics) and fundamental social and economic reform."

Shame

On p. 77 of his book *Without Shame or Fear: From Adam to Christ*, Bishop Rob Hirschfeld states that "shame tells me not only that I have made mistakes that draw me from God's purposes. Shame tells me that *I am* a mistake." Psychologists Jack Danielian and Patricia Gianotti describe shame as a "master emotion"—a psychological state that undergirds other emotions such as anger, fear, and depression."[57]

Thandika describes shame as it relates to racism as the feelings of someone who played the "Race Game" as realizing "the feelings he had discarded in order to form his white identity." This sense of shame is not only about how we interact with others. Further, as Bishop Hirschfeld points out, it is also about a complicity in perpetuating the status quo because of our "silence about cruelty or injustice or abuse rather than experience the discomfort of taking action to reveal decline—afraid we will somehow make the victim, or ourselves even more vulnerable, and amplifying the damage done [to] them (and us)."[58]

Fear

On the subject of fear, Thandika speaks of "children and adults who learned to think of themselves as white to stay out of trouble with their caretakers and in the good graces of their peers or the enforcers of community racial standards. Their motive was not to attack someone outside their own racial community. They simply wanted to remain within their own community— or at least not to be abandoned by it."[59]

Fears leads to intolerance. Fear breeds contempt and stress. Thandika describes clearly how so called "race laws" came into being and created the mechanism for social control that is the cultural narrative for the United States today. I think it is critically important to understand "the distinction between economic and psychological uses of race. And how an "upper-class economic ploy (classism) became a lower-class psychological need (racism). These laws became the standard for laws made in all the colonies, particularly in the South which relied on labor to produce wealth more so than in the North."[60]

The above boils down to a fear of losing "something," even though we may not know what. This results from the Paradox of Diversity.[61] It is also referred to as wanting to win the "zero-sum game"—the assertion that there are finite resources in the world and in any situation where there are two people vying for a resource, only one (me) should get it or I lose. Here's how this was described in a Harvard Business Review article:

> "On the practical side, affirmative action policies designed to increase minority representation may focus Whites' attention on the impact of quota-like procedures on their own access to education and employment, in effect threatening their resources

(Haley & Sidanius, 2006). On the symbolic side, Whites may fear that minorities' imposition of their cultural values represent an attack on White cultural values and norms, as evidenced by Whites' resentment of norms of political correctness (Norton, Sommers, Apfelbaum, Pura, & Ariely, 2006) and the belief of many Whites in a "War on Christians" (Gibson, 2005)."[62]

What do these emotions look like?

Range of Actions

I have created a Diversity Behavior Continuum as a framework to help us understand the range of behavior that can be observed in the expression of bias: see Exhibit 5.7 The Diversity Behavior Continuum.

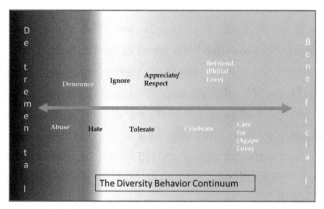

Exhibit 5.7. The Diversity Behavior Continuum

Behavior to the left of the continuum (the red area) shows behavior that is detrimental to a relationship. Behavior to the right of the continuum (the greener area) shows behavior that is beneficial to a relationship.

To internalize the continuum, think about the differences between these behaviors. These are representative of degree of impact:

> ➤ Abusing someone vs denouncing them: Abusing is causing harm to someone. Denouncing is merely stating you think they are a bad person. I do not believe in the adage "Sticks and stones can break my bones but words can never hurt me."

➤ Denouncing someone vs. hating them: Hating is your perception of someone. No one knows about your hate but you. Denouncing is taking action to make a statement against someone.

➤ Ignoring someone vs. tolerating them: Ignoring someone is not acknowledging that they exist. Tolerating someone is acknowledging they exist but not liking them.

➤ Appreciating someone vs. celebrating them: Appreciating someone is understanding who they are. Again, no one knows about your valuing them. Celebrating them is letting others know that you appreciate them.

➤ Befriending someone vs. caring for them: Befriending someone is interacting with them in a casual manner. (The Greeks call this *filial* love.) Caring for someone is engaging them a much deeper level. (The Greeks call this *agape* love.)

We want individual behavior as well as organizational policies, procedures, and processes that put us toward the right of the continuum: appreciate/respect, celebrate, befriend, care for.

Microaggressions

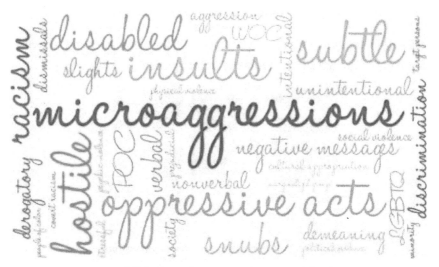

Exhibit 5.8. Microaggressions Wordcloud

Chester M. Pierce first coined the term "microaggression" in the 1970s, as a way to describe the subtle insults and put-downs that African Americans experienced regularly.

There are 3 forms of microaggressions: Verbal, Behavioral, and Environmental.

Psychologist Derald Wing Sue and colleagues defined three types or forms of microaggression (in order of violence):

1. **Microinvalidations:** A microinvalidation is when a person's comment invalidates or undermines the experiences of a certain group of people. An example of a microinvalidation would be a man stating an idea in a meeting as if it were his own, when the same idea was just stated by a woman.

2. **Microinsults:** A microinsult is a comment or action that is unintentionally discriminatory. For example, this could be a hospital administrator saying to an Indian doctor, "Your people must be so proud of you for becoming a doctor."

3. **Microassaults:** A microassault is when a person intentionally behaves in a discriminatory way while not intending to be offensive. An example of a microassault is a person telling a racist joke then saying, "I was just joking."

An article in *American Psychologist* documents 9 flavors of microaggressions, shown in Exhibit 5.9 Nine Flavors of Microaggressions.[63]

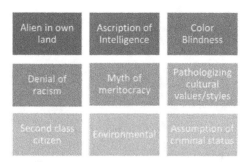

Exhibit 5.9. Nine Flavors of Microaggressions

Some environmental and assumption of criminal status microaggressions can actually be examples of interpersonal or institutional bias.

White Normativeness/White Privilege

These biases stem from and lead to "White Normativity" where our society is built to serve the dominant culture which, in the U.S. is decidedly white[64] and patriarchal. An example I like to use is that of a visitor to a hotel room. When we visit our hotel room, we expect there to be a bathroom. In that bathroom, we have come to expect there to be complimentary soap and shampoo.

But for whose hair was that shampoo designed? Not for a person of color. Now think of all the products and services in the world. How many of them were designed for people of color? In fact, there are some companies that have been formed around creating products and services for those who are melanin-enhanced because most products and services were designed for those who are melanin-diminished.

It is this white normativeness that creates "white privilege"—the societal privilege that benefits white people over non-white people in some societies, particularly if they are otherwise under the same social, political, or economic circumstances. If you are a White person going into a hotel room and expect that the shampoo in the hotel room will work for you, you are experiencing white privilege.

Understanding the dominant culture allows us to truly understand the cause of lack of DEI. Why is this? In her book *Waking Up White*, Debby Irving writes "The purpose of identifying and examining the dominant white culture is not to prove that white people are racist or that everything that white people think and do is wrong. It's a way to provide feedback along the lines of 'Here are some dominant white culture ways of thinking and acting that are holding back efforts to dismantle racism.'"

Here are some examples Irving cites of dominant white culture ways of thinking that you have probably observed in organizations:

- Conflict avoidance
- Valuing formal education over life experience
- Emotional restraint
- Judgmentalism
- Either/or thinking

- ➤ Right to comfort and entitlement
- ➤ Sense of urgency
- ➤ Competitiveness

- ➤ Belief in one right way
- ➤ Defensiveness
- ➤ Being status oriented

These all contribute to lack of DEI.

Lest you think this is a modern-day concept, academics such as Charles V. Hamilton recognized how modern-era European-organized slavery began a centuries-long progression of white privilege and non-white subjugation. For more on these concepts view the video "White Privilege" and read Peggy McIntosh's article "White Privilege: Unpacking the Invisible Knapsack."[65]

Group/Systemic Bias

Systemic (aka group or institutionalized) bias: Cultural norms, best practices, policies, procedures, and laws (local, state, and federal) in an organization or society that force an individual's discriminatory behavior. This term was first coined in 1967 by Stokely Carmichael and Charles V. Hamilton in Black Power: The Politics of Liberation.

One example of systemic bias is a policy of not allowing women into a club. Another example is a policy of not hiring someone who does not have at least a bachelor's degree.

Structural Bias

Structural (aka societal) bias is formalization of a set of institutional, historical, cultural, and interpersonal practices within a society that places one or more social or ethnic groups in a better position to succeed and disadvantages other groups so that disparities develop between the groups over a period of time.[66] Structural bias involves practices or regulations that cross systems—such as:

 Wealth   Healthcare

📺	Media	🎓	Education
🏠	Housing	⚖️	Criminal Justice

An example is pay inequities. As shown in Chapter 2, data shows that women are not paid on par with men in almost all industries.

Key reader takeaways

People make up organizations. The root cause of lack of DEI in organizations is implicit bias in individuals. Implicit bias manifests in many ways: verbal and behavioral. The manifestations occur at multiple levels: interpersonal, systemic, and structural. Recognizing this root cause and how it manifests in establishing white normativeness and white (male) privilege allows us to come up with ways to eliminate those caught.

Consider This...

This chapter explored the causes of lack of DEI.

> ➢ How are you biased? To find out, you can take a Harvard Implicit Association Test here https://implicit.harvard.edu/implicit/takeatest.html.
> ➢ How do you feel when you see a person of color? When you see someone of the opposite sex? When you hear someone espouse a political view different than your own?
> ➢ Where do you see white privilege showing up in your own life, family, or organizations of which you are a member?
> ➢ Where do you see gender discrimination showing up in your own life, family, or organizations of which you are part?

> ➤ How might white privilege work to diminish a group's willingness to hear feedback, handle differences, or be open to multiple points of view?

> ➤ What is the opposite of each of the dominant white culture ways of thinking mentioned earlier, and how can you find ways to bring more balance into your organization? For example, if the culture is highly competitive, how can you bring in more cooperation? Or if people avoid conflict, how can you build skills and processes to deal with conflicts in a generative way?

How does your job or daily activity perpetuate white (male) privilege?

This chapter explored the cause of the lack of equitable inclusion of diverse people in the pursuit of being a high-performing organization. Here are some questions you should ask yourself to see if you are ready to move on:

Question	Your Response
Can you describe what implicit bias is?	
Can you recognize when implicit bias manifests itself?	
Are you willing to commit to de-biasing yourself so you can help lead your organization to better performance using the information provided in this chapter?	

If you answered "yes" to these questions, then you are ready to move on to the next chapter, which explores what diversity has to do with organizational performance.

PART 3

Diversity and Organizational Performance

What diversity has to do with organizational performance and the organizational performance system.

CHAPTER 6

What Does Diversity Have to Do with Organizational Performance?

"There are not more than five musical notes, yet the combinations of these five give rise to more melodies than can ever be heard. There are not more than five primary colours, yet in combination they produce more hues than can ever been seen. There are not more than five cardinal tastes, yet combinations of them yield more flavours than can ever be tasted."

—Sun Tzu

Thesis: *DEI has an impact on efficiency, effectiveness, relevance, and financial viability.*

Organizational Performance
- Effectiveness
- Efficiency
- Relevance
- Financial Viability

Chapter 1 laid out the case for DEI for organizational performance. But how does DEI impact an organizational performance from an operational perspective? Chapter 5 showed that organizations are made of people; thus, the way the organization performs is a direct result of how people in the organization perform.

Let's go back to the definition of organizational performance from Chapter 3 and explore the impact of diversity on organizational performance in more detail. You will recall organizational performance was defined using the Institutional and Organizational Assessment Model (IOA). Let's look at how DEI impacts each of the aspect of that framework.

Effectiveness

You will recall from Chapter 3 that effectiveness has to do with how well an organization fulfills its mission. Take a moment to ask yourself, *what challenges does your organization have regarding effectiveness?*

For example, consider this description:

> "Successful companies like Dewey & Levin, a small public-interest law firm located in a northeastern U.S. city, incorporate employees' perspectives into the main work of the organization and to enhance work by rethinking primary tasks and redefining markets, products, strategies, missions, business practices, and even cultures. Such companies are using the learning-and-effectiveness paradigm for managing diversity and, by doing so, are tapping diversity's true benefits."[67]

For each process in the organization, we should seek to leverage the different ideas and capabilities that a diverse set of people can bring to bear.

Efficiency

You will recall from Chapter 3 that efficiency has to do with getting the most out of resources available in fulfilling the organization's mission. Take a moment to ask yourself, *what challenges does your organization have regarding efficiency?*

As stated in Chapter 1, research shows that having diversity and the teamwork of an organization are significant predictors of organizational efficiency. Having diversity and the management of that diversity and the teamwork are significant predictors of organizational efficiency. "Diversity has the unique ability to display different perspectives and when those different perspectives are applied in the workplace the result is a more efficient and humane work environment with empathy, understanding, and responsibility as core values."[68]

As Aura Huot of Levalee Brensinger Architects says, "People are in the organization to do a great job, when people feel engaged, valuable, and appreciated. And when we contribute to their development, people are going to do more."

Let's move on now to relevance.

Relevance

You will recall from Chapter 3 that relevance has to do with whether clients and customers find that an organization's programs, products, or services address their needs or wants over time. Furthermore, long-term relevance is about continually revising and improving products and services to meet clients' needs—adapting the mission of the organization to continue to meet stakeholders' needs, which can evolve over time. This also involves adapting to the environment in which you're operating, and keeping a good reputation. Take a moment to consider, *what challenges does your organization have regarding relevance?*

Chapter 1 described two parts to relevance: product/service (brand) relevance and organizational relevance. Let's look at how diversity plays a role in each.

Product/Service (Brand) Relevance

Chapter 3 discussed that product or service (brand) relevance has to do with four factors (as depicted in Exhibit 3.4): sensory, thinking, values, and community, described in the following subsections.

Sensory and Thinking

The desired user experience and the need or increasing the convenience of the consumer of a product and service can have many functions/

characteristics. Having an engaged diverse workforce improves the chances that you will be able to identify and implement a greater percentage of those functions/characteristics in ways that are effective for the consumer.

According to *HR Magazine:*

> "Age-diverse groups, with different experiences, exercise communication and understanding more than non-diverse groups. Consequently, empathy translates not only in better internal communication but also towards the relationship between company and customer. Empathy translates to a better understanding of the target audience of the company and essentially increased sales."[69]

An example of where not having a DEI mindset caused issues with a product is facial recognition software. There have been several news stories over the past few years highlighting the fact that facial recognition software does not accurately identify African-Americans. The reason for this is twofold: first, the databases of facial features used by the companies who built that software include very few African-Americans; second, the leaders of the development teams were not sensitive to diversity and either did not understand the notion of white normativeness—or they did not care about it. Either way, the products are now recognized as not performing as advertised and the names of the companies producing the software have a tarnished reputation.

Values

The values of customers/clients are diverse. Having an engaged diverse workforce improves the chances that you will be able to understand those values, and build them into your product/service. An article in *HR Magazine* sums this up well:

> "...the inclusion of mature workers in the workplace can offer the company a wide range of experience, knowledge, and resources that can be used to navigate an array of tasks and situations in an effective and time-efficient manner. Workers with diverse

experiences can significantly improve many aspects of a company, from the inner processes to customer support to product development. People with experience have tried and true business techniques that will increase the value of your company's services."[70]

Community

The desire to be associated with a product or service comes from when the organization that produces it has a reputation that is favorable. Marketing can only go so far to build a product's or service's reputation. It takes diverse customers and clients who are willing to vouch for it to increase the chances it will resonate with as many people as possible. In addition, many organizations now only want to do business with suppliers who focus on DEI. This seems to be particularly true in the legal profession and in large manufacturing companies.

Organizational Relevance

Clients and customers change. The community in which you operate changes. Things don't stand still. Thus, awareness of the changing needs of clients and customers, the community, and employees must constantly change.

In the face of these changes, some argue "Why change if it's worked before?" Innovation is change. As mentioned in Chapter 1, Vijay S. Rawan (executive chairman of the Chi Group of Companies) stated that diversity is key for disruption and innovation. He reflects the research showing that bringing together people of different ethnicities with different experiences is a key driver of innovation.

Think about the companies that you consider most innovative—such as Apple, Google, Tesla. They all have very diverse workforces. And they are very innovative because of that.

The World Forum article discussed in Chapter 1 talked about the most innovative, disruptive and prosperous urban centers in the world – New

York, Dubai, London, and Singapore – they all have one thing in common: they are all international melting pots with a high concentration of immigrants. Research shows that there is a direct correlation between high-skilled immigration and an increase in the level of innovation and economic performance in cities and regions. This contributes to those aspects of relevance we discussed.

Jannine Skinner, a senior engineer and member of the DEI Committee at Atos, shared that Atos is "trying to get a lot of women in the scientific community because they realize that there is a lot of untapped knowledge and potential."

Nannan Hu, founder and former executive at Greenhouse Software, said that because of the diversity in their organization:

> "I think we were able to innovate faster, we were able to debate more perspectives and more angles. And we were ultimately able to better serve our customers, because we had a diverse workplace, right, both in terms of ethnicity, gender, socio-economic background....[it was evident that] a homogenous group of folks would not have come up with those innovations... I think you're leaving a lot on the table in terms of being able to capture the most innovative idea. So, I think diversity from all those perspectives is critical to high performing organizations."

Armando Llorente, also a People & Culture Consultant for SHRN (the Senior Human Resources Network), shared with me the story of one company's ability to incubate and foster ideas and new product applications as a result of multiple perspectives from individuals with different educational backgrounds or life backgrounds, coming into a team and, and being able to interact with one another effectively, and then to be able to move ahead when they identified a breakthrough idea. He said, "A (Latino-American) software developer that came up with a solution to a patch that had been problematic, and lo and behold, his idea was the fix. And suddenly, it became an opportunity for others to see, well, if Cesaro spoke up and had this impact on the business, it must be okay for me to come up with my ideas or my feedback or my constructive commentary about what's going on?"

In Chapter 1, we discussed the "Millennial Quotient"—the notion that by the year 2025, 75% of the global workforce will be made up of millennials— which means this group will occupy the majority of leadership roles over the coming decade. Chapter 3 discussed the different desires and perspectives of people from different generations. Different experiences, different backgrounds and different perspectives is what drives innovation and keeps an organization relevant over time.

Relevance in terms of values – not only the product but the brand of the company stands for the same things I do. That drives customer loyalty.

Financial Viability

You will recall from Chapter 3 that viability has to do with profitability and having reliable funding sources. Take a moment to think, *what challenges does your organization have with financial viability?*

Chapter 3 established that having diversity of opinion makes for better decisions because of access to more perspectives. This applies to all of the Financial Planning Factors shown in Exhibit 3.5:

➢ *Risk management is* identifying risks, developing risk-mitigation strategies, and implementing those strategies when risks thresholds are reached. The more perspectives you have, the better your risk identification; the better your risk mitigation strategies; and the better the implementation of those strategies.

➢ *Valuation of a company* is the analytical process of determining the current (or projected) worth of a company. The more perspectives you have, the better your understanding of the company, who would value it, and what value they would place on it.

➢ *Valuation of assets* is the analytical process of determining the current (or projected) worth of assets. The more perspectives you have, the better your understanding of the assets, who would value them, and what value they would place on them.

➢ *Mergers and acquisitions* are transactions in which the ownership of companies, other business organizations, or their operating units are transferred or consolidated with other entities. The more perspectives you have, the better the analysis of the capabilities and potential of the entities in question to determine whether the entities should be joined. The more perspectives you have, the better the recommendations around how the entity that should be joined.

➢ *Option pricing* is the process of identifying a price for the stock of a company. The more perspectives you have, the better you will understand the market potential and the better your pricing will be.

➢ *Budget and forecasting* is a three-step strategic planning process for determining and detailing an organization's long- and short-term financial goals. The more perspectives you have, the more accurate the budgeting and forecasting.

➢ *Capital allocation* is distributing and investing a company's financial resources in ways that will increase its efficiency and maximize its profits. The more perspectives you have, the better you will understand where capital is needed and how best to distribute it.

➢ *Raising capital* is the process a business goes through in order to raise money, so the business can get off the ground, expand, or transform in some way. The more perspectives you have, the more you will be able to connect with the holders of various sources of capital. And since more and more funders are looking for organizations that focus on DEI, adding a focus on it makes you more attractive to them.

Key reader takeaways

Organizations that are diverse are more innovative. Organizations that are diverse are more productive. Organizations that are diverse come up with better solutions to problems. Organizations that are diverse make better decisions.

If you have diverse people in your organization, you can know better what is relevant for a wider market base. You can better understand your stakeholders' needs. Diverse staff can help with your reputation in the marketplace. Diversity can help improve financial viability, as shown in studies by McKinsey and others.

Consider This...

This chapter explored what DEI has to do with organizational performance from multiple perspectives.

Efficiency:

➤ What are the levels of increase of productivity?
➤ Is your organization meeting clients' expectations?

Effectiveness:

➤ Are the functions within your organization meeting expectation of the other functions in the organization?
➤ Does your organization have a wide range of perspectives in your decision making?
➤ Are you efficiently producing your products and services?

Relevance:

➤ Are your products, services, and programs continuing to be relevant to your clients and those you are serving?
➤ Is your organization meeting all stakeholder needs?
➤ Is your reputation good? In your industry? In your markets?

Financial viability:

➤ Is your organization sustainable in terms of its operations?
➤ Is your organization profitable?

> ➤ Does your organization have reliable, ongoing funding sources?

This chapter described how DEI improves organizational performance conceptually. Here are some questions you should ask yourself to see if you are ready to move on:

Question	Your Response
Do you understand how DEI impacts effectiveness?	
Do you understand how DEI impacts efficiency?	
Do you understand how DEI impacts relevance?	
Do you understand how DEI impacts financial viability?	

If you answered "yes" to these questions, then you are ready to move on to the next chapter, which describes the impact diversity has on the organizational performance system.

CHAPTER 7

How Does Diversity Impact the Organizational Performance System?

"Diversity: the art of thinking independently together."
—Malcolm Forbes

Thesis: *DEI has an impact on the Organizational Performance System as defined by Curt Howes: stakeholder value delivery, technical core competencies, and financials.*

In his book <u>Organizational Performance: The Key to Success in the 21ˢᵗ Century,</u> Curt J. Howes describes the organizational performance system shown in Exhibit 7.1. I like this model better than other models such as the McKinsey 7S Model because those other models tend to focus on non-technical/non-operational aspects which, when considering long-term organizational performance, can be impacted by the operational aspects of an organization.

Let's look at how DEI can impact each of the three levels shown in Exhibit 7.1.

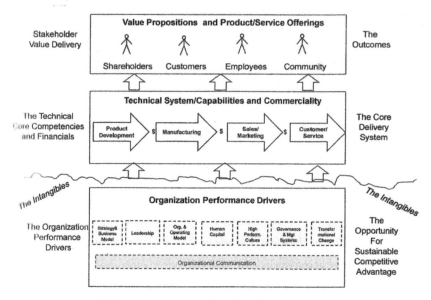

Exhibit 7.1. Organizational Performance System

Stakeholder Value Delivery (Level 1)

Howes says that stakeholder value delivery is about the core purpose of an organization. The outcome of the work of the organization should be to deliver products and services (product/service offerings) in such a way (the value proposition) that brings value to the stakeholders, customers, employees, and community in which your organization operates.

To understand how DEI impacts stakeholder value delivery, let's explore Howes' two-step process of developing a value proposition.

> ➢ **Understand what customers and other stakeholders value.**
> This has to do with the organizational performance aspect of relevance we discussed in Chapter 6's section on sensory and thinking. Having diverse perspectives in an organization doing this work provides a better understanding of the needs of a broader set of customers and stakeholders. As an example, a man cannot possibly know, from his own experience, what products or services a woman needs or wants during a pregnancy.

➤ **Translate that value proposition into products and services that create an experience the customers and other stakeholders value.** This has to do with the organizational performance aspects of effectiveness and relevance we discussed in Chapter 6. Having diverse perspectives in an organization doing this work provides a better understanding of what customers and stakeholders find valuable and how the product/service will actually meet the need. To carry forth the previous example, a man cannot possibly know, from his own experience, what products or services a woman will actually pay for or whether they will be effective during a pregnancy.

Technical Core Competencies & Financials (Level 2)

Howes says that Technical Core Competencies & Financials are about having "an effective technical system and capabilities to deliver it to value proposition through high-quality products and services."[71] The outputs of this level have to do with the organizational performance aspects discussed in the previous chapter's sections on Efficiency and Financial Viability.

To understand how DEI impacts Technical Core Competencies and Financials, let's look at the four technical core competencies of the Core Delivery System:

➤ **Product/Service Development.** More perspectives increase the chance that the features and functions of the product or service will be relevant to a larger customer or client base. More perspectives bring more innovation: better ideas for how features and functions should be implemented and delivered to the customer or client for the most customer/client impact. This results in increased effectiveness of the product/service. For example, a disabled person on a product test team will bring a true understanding of the use of a product or service by disabled customers, whereas an able-bodied tester would only be guessing and likely to miss problems that a disabled person might encounter with the product or service.

➤ **Manufacturing.** More perspectives bring more innovation: better ideas for efficiency of the manufacturing process. This includes supply chain management as well as order fulfillment. This results in increased effectiveness of the manufacturing process.

➤ **Sales/marketing.** More perspectives increase the relevance of the marketing campaigns and sales pitches. Consider Sony's "Racist" ad promoting its white PlayStation Portable device: Sony decided to promote the new product with a pale woman with white hair grabbing a black woman by the face. The white figure looks upset and determined while the black figure looks very submissive. The text reads "PlayStation Portable. White is Coming." There are so many better ways to promote the launch of your new product. Sony was quoted as saying, "The images that were used in the campaign were intended solely to highlight the contrast between the different colors available for the PSP." Whomever made the final decision to go with the ad was insensitive to how it would be perceived. If there had been a person of color on the advertising team the odds would have been increased that the ad would not have gone public.[72]

➤ **Customer/Service.** More perspectives increase the organization's ability to understand its customers or clients when they call in for need assistance. For example, during the 1980s, many U.S. companies began outsourcing their customer service hotlines to companies in India. This was done, presumably, to save money. What these companies did not realize is that most customers want to speak with someone who speaks with an American English accent. The issue was not that the service provided by the Indian support representatives was necessarily any worse than the service provided by native American-English speakers. But in the customer service world, from the customer's perspective, the

Customer Service Representative is the company. And if the customer cannot understand the customer service representatives, then the perception is that the company does not understand the needs of the customer. In the end, many companies lost customers and have, actually, switched back to native American-English speaking customer service representatives.

To further understand how DEI impacts, let's explore the five areas Howes says are important in designing the technical system. (Execution in these areas span and support all of the four core competencies listed above).

> **Defining the technical requirements for a business or industry segment**. As every industry has its own way of doing things, naturally, some people will be more skilled at operating one way and others in a different way. Different industries require different types of work. Different skills and abilities lend themselves to different types of work. For example, manufacturing companies are very process oriented. People who gravitate to a logical thinking style excel in this industry. Whereas people who are consultants excel if they gravitate to a practical thinking style.

> **Knowing the key performance requirements for products and services.** As we have already mentioned, having diverse perspectives in an organization doing this work provides a better understanding of the needs of a broader set of customers and stakeholders.

> The story of the Ford Edsel is a prime example of not understanding key performance requirements for a car: "Ugly, overpriced, overhyped, poorly made and poorly timed, the Edsel was made for only two years. In the end, the failed program cost Ford $250 million [source: Carlson]. The 'car of the future' is now a cautionary tale in business classrooms…"[73]

> **Mapping the technical-work processes.** Benjamin Franklin is credited with saying "If you fail to plan, you plan to fail." As a

project manager, I am acutely aware that projects are most successful when they are planned using project-scheduling methodologies. The same is true for operations of an organization. Work goes more smoothly when everyone knows what they need to do, when they need to do it, and how the need to do it. (You may recall we discussed this in the section on efficiency.) I have observed there is a tendency to forgo planning because the work seems to be "very simple." This attitude frequently is a recipe for failure, causing more work than would have been necessary if planning were done in the first place. A prime example of this is Knight Capital, which was "brought on to work on new code for a new SEC program. an over-optimistic deadline caused them to go to production with test code. After production, a glitch cost the company $440 million within the first 30 minutes of trading, and company stock fell 75% within just two days. Lesson learned, you need a granular-level view of your projects to forecast how long a project will feasibly take to complete and avoid setting unrealistic targets or deadlines."[74]

➤ **Identifying the technical capabilities and key positions required.** Technical capabilities are the resources an organization can bring to bear to develop and deliver products and services. Identifying key positions required for superior organizational performance is about workforce planning: having the right people with the right skills at the right place at doing the right job at the right time.

(You may recall, we discussed this in the section on efficiency.) A simple example of this is if you need to advertise a new product, you don't have the engineers develop the advertising campaign; instead, you plan upfront to have people available with advertising skills and experience.

➤ **Setting the measures of technical excellence.** H. Thomas Johnson, American accounting historian, and Professor of Business

Administration at Portland State University, is quoted as saying "Perhaps what you measure is what you get. More likely, what you measure is all you'll get. What you don't (or can't) measure is lost." Creating measures of technical excellence is all about accountability. This circles back to what we discussed in the Chapter 6 section on effectiveness. Having diverse perspectives provides better identification of goals and measures. It also provides more accurate estimates of whether goals (technical and financial) are realistic.

Organizational Performance Drivers (Level 3)

Organizational Performance Drivers are about the principles and behaviors that should be used in the execution of the core delivery system. To understand how DEI impacts the organizational performance drivers, let's look at them one by one.

Strategy And the Business Model. This driver was described by Michael Porter in his book *Competitive Strategy*: it involves considering the "5 Forces".

Creating the strategy and the business model are accomplished by the senior executives of the organization. You may recall that Chapter 1 described the benefits of a senior executive team that is diverse.

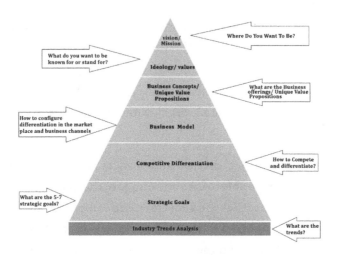

Exhibit 7.2 Strategy-Development Process

To understand how DEI impacts creating the strategy and business model, let's look at the elements of Howes' strategy-development process as depicted in Exhibit 7.2:

- ➢ **Industry Trends Analysis** is better done by people with diverse perspectives as they are better able to understand a wide variety of trends occurring.
- ➢ **Strategic Goals** are more ambitious and realistic when created by people with diverse perspectives.
- ➢ **Competitive Differentiation** is greater when people with different perspectives are involved who can articulate the needs and desires of a wider variety of audiences as a result of a wide variety of perspectives.
- ➢ **Business Model** identification can be more innovative and accurate if performed by people with a wide variety of perspectives.
- ➢ **Business Concepts/Unique Value Propositions** were discussed in the section on Stakeholder Value Delivery, earlier in this chapter.
- ➢ **Ideology/Values** were also discussed in the section on stakeholder value delivery earlier in this chapter.
- ➢ **Vision/Mission** were also discussed in the section on relevance in Chapter 6.

Leadership. As Howes says, "Leaders are the architects of performance that drive all other dimensions."[75] He goes on to say that "two traits separate really great leaders from good ones: 1) the ability to see opportunities and risks that others don't see, and 2) the ability to mobilize the resources and the overall organizational systems to execute a performance."

If an organization is not diverse and leaders are not inclusive, the organization will not be able to take advantage of the many perspectives of a diverse employee base that will allow for more completely and accurately seeing opportunities and risks. If leaders do not act equitably, they lose the trust of their employees and the ability to mobilize resources, which is a major contributor to the Great Resignation we are seeing in companies all across the country.

Organizational and Operating Model is, as Howes says, "a broad vision of how an organization should operate, what the key roles and core functions are, and how the roles and functions interrelate. This vision includes the roles at the corporate level as well as the roles, functions, and the linkages within and across the divisions and departments."[76] If you see an organization with multiple departments duplicating work, you are looking at an organization whose organization and operating model are, probably, deficient. (An exception to this might be if management is following Peter Senge's approach described in The Fifth Discipline to product development where two teams are purposeful assigned the same problem to solve.) Without inclusion of diverse people in an organization, there are few, if any linkages between functions within or across an organization.

Human Capital is all about the talent lifecycle: the ability to attract, hire, develop, motivate, and retain talent. Notice I did not describe *employees*; I used the word *talent*. This is because a human capital strategy can also include acquiring services from a supplier rather than hiring someone as an employee.

This element is the crux of DEI. It is how you bring diversity into the organization and equitably include that diversity through HR principles and processes That encourages work that brings the organizational performance we have been discussing. (This is discussed much more detail in Chapter 15.)

High-performance Culture is, as Howes says, "the sustainability of desired performance."[77] The culture of the organization needs to create an environment such that people not only know how to behave and interact, but also want to come to work every day and perform at their best.

Culture involves defining the principles and values that guide the organization. The more those principles and values resonate with employees, the more they will be motivated to work at their utmost. Whether we admit it or not, our organizations do have at least some diversity as defined by the Diversity Wheel. So, our principles and values need to be articulated in such a way as to reach a diverse group of employees. If those principles and values don't resonate with employees, they will not feel included or valued. This lack of resonating with an organization's culture is another factor in the Great Resignation movement we are seeing.

Chapter 6 and this chapter discussed the impact of DEI on the effectiveness of the organization (achieving the organization's mission) and the efficiency of the organization (the productivity of the organization in using its resources) which, in the end, is the desired high performance.

Governance And Management Systems are about, as Howes says, "ensuring safe, legal, and reliable performance that can be tracked, measured, and effectively managed for risk."[78] The systems are made up of three primary levels:

➤ **Corporate advisory boards** – we have already talked about fact that diverse senior leadership needs to a greater likelihood of organizational performance better than your peers;

➤ **Performance and risk management systems** – we have already talked about the impact of DEI on risk management;

➤ **Policies and complaints assessment** – policies that are not inclusive or equitable lead to an environment where employees do not feel welcome or as if they belong. And we've already discussed what happens when employees feel unwelcome or if they do not belong. We've also already talked about tracking and measuring performance in terms of accountability in the section on Technical Core Competencies & Financials.

Organization Transformation is changing the behavior of an organization. Exhibit 7.4 shows steps for leaders to create sustainable change, with how DEI impacts each step.

Change Step	Impact of DEI
Establish a sense of urgency.	Different people are motivated by different things. The sense of urgency needs to be established in a way that motivates different people.
Form a powerful guiding coalition.	The coalition (by definition) means people from different areas or functions. Bringing different people together is an act of inclusion.
Create a vision.	A good vision speaks to many different people from many different perspectives. Thus, many perspectives are needed to craft a vision that speaks to diverse people with different perspectives. Vision creation benefits from following the three methods of rhetoric identified by Aristotle: ethos, pathos, and logos.
Communicate the vision.	Different people understand concepts in different ways. Some people learn and comprehend better visually, some auditorily, some kinesthetically, some textually. Communicating a vision must be executed to account for those different ways.
Empower others to act on the vision.	Empowering people is including them. As we have seen previously, the more perspectives involved in executing tasks, the better chance of innovation, efficiency, and effectiveness.
Plan for and create short-term wins.	Some people are motivated by small celebrations. For example, people who gravitate to practical thinking respond well to checking tasks off a list of such as short-term wins.
Consolidate improvements and produce even more change.	DEI has no real impact on this.
Institutionalize the approaches.	DEI has no real impact on this.

Exhibit 7.4. Steps to Creating Sustainable Change[79]

Organizational Communication needs to, as Howes says, span across all organizational boundaries, provide timely information, encourage collaboration, and connect please and leaders to a common purpose. Some have said that people are the organs of an organization and communication is the lifeblood of the organization. As stated in Exhibit 7.4, different people can understand concepts in different ways. So, communication must be executed to account for those different ways.

There are many assessment tools that can identify different learning and comprehension styles. Several are described on the verywellmind site.[80]

Key reader takeaways

The three levels of the Organizational Performance System (stakeholder value delivery, technical core competencies and financials, and organizational performance drivers) are impacted by DEI. Stakeholder Value Delivery includes the identification of products and/or services that stakeholders of the organization would find valuable. Identification of such products and/or services is easier and much more accurate if performed by people with diverse perspectives.

Technical Core Competencies and Financials includes the actual work of developing and delivering the organization's products and/or services. This is also referred to as the Core Delivery System. Innovation, efficiency, development and delivery are enhanced when people with different perspectives is our being equitably included in that work.

Operation Performance Drivers are the principles and behaviors that should be used in the execution of the Core Delivery System. Research has proven that equitable inclusion of diverse people encouraged by established principles and values (i.e., culture) lead to the behaviors necessary to achieve superior organizational performance.

Consider This...

This chapter explored how DEI impacts of the organizational performance system.

- ➤ Does your organization have a value proposition that resonates with as diverse an audience as it could?
- ➤ Have you considered how DEI improves your organization's Core Delivery System?
- ➤ Do your organizational communications follow Aristotle's advice for rhetoric?

This chapter described how DEI impacts the Organizational Performance System. Here are some questions you should ask yourself to see if you are ready to move on:

Question	Your Response
Do you understand Howes' Organizational Performance System at a high level?	
Do you understand how DEI impacts the three levels of Organizational Performance System?	

If you answered "yes" to these questions, then you are ready to move on to the next chapter, which looks at the barriers and challenges to igniting superior organizational performance through diversity.

PART 4

Preparing to Ignite Superior Organizational Performance Through Diversity

Challenges to achieving organizational performance through diversity, the signs of DEI and levers that can be pulled to make DEI happen, and the Roadmap to Discovering Performance Through Diversity follows the Plan-Do-Check-Act Cycle.

CHAPTER 8

What Are the Challenges to Igniting Organizational Performance Through Diversity

"Inclusivity means not just 'we're allowed to be there,' but we are valued. I've always said: smart teams will do amazing things, but truly diverse teams will do impossible things."
—Claudia Brind-Woody

Thesis: *It is important to recognize the challenges to organizational performance through diversity so they can be overcome.*

This chapter describes challenges to achieving organizational performance through diversity, equity, and inclusion. It does so by describing the concerns about DEI, the myths about DEI and the challenges in implementing a DEI program followed by describing the challenges an organization can expect to face if diversity alone has been achieved without equitable or inclusive behaviors being established as the expected norm. These challenges impact all four aspects of organizational performance.

Concerns

There are many concerns expressed about having a diverse organization. Here are some of the most common concerns revealed during surveys and interviews in which I have been involved.

Fear of Mission Drift

Leaders are committed to fulfilling the primary mission of their organization. They are concerned that integrating DEI will pull them off-purpose, thereby stretching their limited human and financial resources.

However, the reality is DEI will help ensure the purpose of the organization is being fulfilled as the organization will better understand the needs and wants of customers or those being served will be better.

Lack of knowledge

While leaders are confident that they understand the mission of their organizations and capacity needs that are core to achieving that mission, they do not feel they have sufficient knowledge and understanding of DEI issues to determine capacity needs in this area. Leaders acknowledge that they don't know enough about DEI to know where to begin addressing it within their organizations. An example of this is where an HR Director for a small hospital shared that "Clinicians are great, but they have been put into management roles and are poor managers. There is no management development program."

The reality is summed up well by Aura Huot, Director of People & Culture at Lavallee Brensinger Architects who shared with me:

> "There is a misunderstanding of what DEI really is. People start shutting off when they hear DEI. We have not been educated

enough to understand what diversity is and what are the attributes. People don't know what equity means and what inclusion means. Not having an understanding of those definitions prevents efforts from being successful... One of the greatest feedback items I received in a training was from a person who said they were not aware of the discrimination."

Discomfort with DEI

Most leaders self-identify as being from dominant social groups (e.g., in terms of race/ethnicity, gender, socioeconomic status, educational attainment, etc.) and express a level of discomfort with leading DEI efforts, especially as it relates to race and ethnicity. Based on aspects of self-identity, they feel they don't have permission to do the work of integrating diversity, equity, and inclusion into their ongoing mission-driven enterprises.

Leaders interviewed identified the need for greater racial/ethnic diversity as a priority and would rely on people of color—for example, who are on staff, serve on the board, or otherwise are engaged with the organization— to solve the problem of addressing DEI issues. Discomfort can also cause leaders to ignore DEI issues or minimize the extent to which they matter, allowing organizations to continue operating as usual without explicitly addressing DEI.

However, in reality, having a "Growth Mindset" (as described by Carol Dweck at Stanford University) is important so that all can overcome this discomfort. Yet, as the HR Director of a major hospital shared with me, "People don't have the Growth Mindset."

Reverse Discrimination

Leaders expressed concern that if they gave preference to people in the non-dominant group, they would be accused of discrimination against people in the dominant group. Recent Affirmative Action cases such as that about admissions practices at Harvard University[81] show this is a tricky subject worthy of concern.

However, in reality, Anastasia Reesa Tomkin describes "The Case for Selective Discrimination" through the case of David Duvall who filed an unlawful termination lawsuit against Novant Health after being fired citing racial and gender discrimination as a white man. A federal jury of his peers in North Carolina agreed with Duvall's perception of events and made history this October by awarding the former Senior Vice President of Marketing and Communications $10 million for his troubles. She states "after generations of white supremacist policies overtly or covertly excluding people of color from socioeconomic advantages instituted by the government, white people are so eager to label any and all remedies as "racial discrimination" ... if some white people are not replaced by people of color in leadership positions, there won't be diverse leadership. If people of color are not hired, there won't be diverse staff. Amending the insidious discrimination of the past to any significant degree will not be achieved through neutrality or colorblindness. It will be achieved through prioritizing and empowering those who have been disempowered and sidelined for so long."[82]

Myths

Effective efforts to address diversity, equity, and inclusion (DEI) within an organization benefit from discerning myth from reality and operating under clear and explicit assumptions.

The DEI journey that organizations are eager to begin or continue will require leaders to be aware of how misconceptions can cloud reality. Leaders must be willing to confront underlying assumptions about what DEI means for the organization and the people it serves. DEI work, when meaningful and effective, might implicate the individuals and longstanding structures within which people have operated for years. Unwrapping and revealing previously unacknowledged expectations and assumptions is important when embarking on the DEI journey.

Organizations operate with several underlying assumptions that are unique to the independent sector, though some may be more evident in the public and private for-profit sectors.

Based on my own research and research performed by Talmira Hill of the T.L. Hill Group, here are 9 myths that seem to prevent DEI initiatives from being successful.

Myth #1: *"Bringing diverse people into an organization over those from the dominant culture amounts to a zero-sum game where there are winners and losers."*

Reality: This assumption is very closely related to the reverse-discrimination concern discussed above. It may be helpful to approach this myth from two perspectives: short-term and long-term.

In the short-term, when there is a choice between two people (say, a man and a woman) for access to a unique resource or position, obviously there can be only one "winner." This is a reality I believe many people choose to ignore or choose not to discuss. However, a short-term view does not usually explain the full situation. This is where the long-term view comes in.

Over the long term, we must think about what we want to achieve in the community or society at large. If overall we want to reduce or eliminate the disparities in pay, for example, between men and women (where there is an historic disparity in favor of men) and there is a limited budget with which to compensate employees in an organization, then giving more of a raise to a woman will seem as a short-term loss for the man. But, in reality, it is changing societal disparity so that everyone wins – moving toward the goal of eliminating pay disparities.

In addition, in the long-term, a short-term loser could also end up winning. Salesforce.com is a company where founder and CEO Mark Bennioff made a commitment to gender pay equity. Some male employees did not get the raises they wanted at the expense of bringing women's pay to parity (i.e., that's a short-term loss for men). But the company's reputation soared and its revenue is allowing it to compensate employees of both genders better than its competition.

Myth #2: *"Ours is a mission-driven organization, so we carry out our commitment to fairness and equity in our ongoing work."*

Reality: This assumption can make it more challenging for leaders and members of organizations to consider the fact that structural bias and inequity are inherent in any organization that does not explicitly, intentionally, and actively work to dismantle it. Not only are organizations made of people who are implicitly biased, they operate within systems that are biased.

Myth #3: "Our mission is to improve opportunities for marginalized groups, so we are reaching some diverse people and communities."

Reality: This assumption reflects the "if we build it, they will come" mentality and often precludes taking intentional and systematic steps within the organization to gather and analyze quantitative and/or qualitative data about who is being served relative to demographic data about who lives in the targeted communities.

This assumption might acknowledge service to one marginalized group without taking into account other types of diversity (as discussed in Chapter 4: What is Diversity?).

Myth #4: "Our organization works within an area that is not diverse. We're predominantly White, so why is this relevant?"

Reality: This line of thinking usually refers to *racial* diversity and, in many cases, ignores data about the changing demographics of almost all geographies which indicate increasing racial/ethnic diversity (as described in Chapter 2). It also overlooks other types of diversity (e.g., age, gender identity, sexual orientation, faith/religious beliefs, ability/disability status, socioeconomic status, among others). This assumption fails to acknowledge the inherent value of diverse perspectives.

Myth #5: "The leaders (including board and executive staff members) of our organization are well-meaning and not biased."

Reality: Although many well-meaning people think they are not biased, all people have implicit bias we are not aware of on a conscious level – by definition, it is unconscious.

It is a good start to mean well, but if that is where the commitment begins and ends, it is highly likely that the organization is not diverse, equitable, or inclusive in its work. Addressing DEI requires intentionality; without it, the status quo ("business as usual") will reflect structural and systemic inequities.

Myth #6: **"Our organization has been fulfilling its mission and has never been accused of discrimination, bias, or not being welcoming or accessible; it's not been a problem for us."**

Reality: Often, people of diverse backgrounds and experiences do not attempt to avail themselves of services by organizations that are not actively taking steps to welcome and include them. Therefore, an organization may not be experiencing a problem because entire groups of potential audiences are not interested in getting to know what they have to offer. Diverse groups don't see themselves reflected, so they are less likely to consider connecting with the organization. Additionally, the organization may not have appropriate systems in place (e.g., grievance procedures and language/communication access) to capture the unhappy experiences and feedback from people who feel they are not well-served by the organization. In this instance, the adage "You don't know what you don't know," is appropriate. Without actively learning about DEI, people and organizations will be unaware of its biases and blind spots.

Organizations seeking to thrive, as opposed to meeting minimal requirements for legal compliance with regard to nondiscrimination, are aware that diverse organizations are more innovative and perform better. Addressing systems of oppression takes all of us. If we want to undo the harms of inequity, then we must all see ourselves in the work and create the change we would like to see.

Myth #7: **"Our organization would like to have more diverse leadership (board and staff), but we live in a White area, and it's impossible to recruit People of Color (PoC) to fill these positions."**

Reality: This assumes that diversity is only about race and ethnicity. Your area has diversity of all types, including racial/ethnic, gender and sexual orientation, age, disability status, geographic location, income level, among others.

Also, this assumes you can recruit only from the area in which you live. Organizations are encouraged to explore, recruit, hire, retain, and promote diverse individuals of all intersectional identities from outside your geographic area. In addition, there are likely organizations in your area that are developing a pipeline of PoC leaders and leaders of diverse backgrounds who are eager to refer them to organizations seeking to attract people of diverse backgrounds.

Myth #8: **"Hiring a Black/Indigenous People of Color (BIPOC) leader will solve DEI issues within our organization."**

Reality: One person cannot and should not be expected to address DEI in an organization unless that person is the DEI Director. Individuals from BIPOC communities can bring perspectives from their lived experiences. The same can be said about a woman or any of the dimensions of personality. Even with a DEI Director, the entire leadership must drive and share ownership for DEI in the organization.

Renowned training metrics thought leaders Jim Kirkpatrick and Wendy Kirkpatrick describe this as: "A big reason DEI initiatives will not be successful with one individual at the helm is because the required drivers package needs support in all areas. Companies cannot hold one person responsible for every employee doing the right thing on the job. And by the same token, one person cannot support and hold accountable every employee." Meaning, one person cannot drive the entire package of projects or tasks to implement DEI by themselves.

Leadership, direction, and support are required at *all* levels of an organization that seeks to address DEI as part of its mission-driven work. DEI efforts operating in isolation or in the absence of collaboration throughout the organization are proven to be less effective.

"Myth #9: **"DEI is expensive. We do not have the resources to address it."**

Reality: There is an organizational cost *not* to address DEI. Those costs include lost quality, lost customers, lost creativity and ingenuity, and lost opportunities to engage with a wider range of communities, particularly those that are underserved.

There are a number of options to consider when determining how to adequately invest in this work. Cost will always be a factor, but it does not need to be a barrier. We did not create or design these systems, but we are responsible for addressing them.

There also are several steps organizations can take that require little or no cost. For example, examining and then changing policies and procedures within the organization to be more centered on equity would be a worthwhile investment, and there are ways to access technical assistance that may cost little or nothing. Sending staff members to DEI workshops can be inexpensive. See the Bonus section at the end of this book for an example.

Ensuring that a Board of Directors is diverse and reflective of the constituencies served is both strategic and inexpensive.

There is undeniable evidence that equitable and inclusive practices lead to heightened levels of organizational innovation, orientation towards service, employee engagement and retention.

Speaking of costs, Denise Lamoreaux of Atos shared with me:

> "...we've probably spent less than $1,000 in 2021 on awards, applications, ..., because I'm being very careful with my spend. But [in terms of the] return on investment, ...when we are in RFPs and a potential client asks what our diversity efforts include, we can point to the awards.... there's a specific document that I produce every year, my year-end review of what happened in the diversity space that really tells our stories.... And...there is a little checkbox that...salespeople...check off when they're doing their review of what really attracted the client and how we won the business. And diversity and inclusion initiatives are included

there. So, you know, many of them do check that box. And I can't say that it's the only reason why a particular client goes with our company. But it has been a contributing factor in several large deals that we've won over the past five years, that would account for millions of dollars, but it's not the only reason; it's a contributing factor."

Challenges

Challenges/barriers at the organizational level make it difficult for the organization to exhibit equitable inclusion of diverse people. Barriers that impede improvements in all four aspects of organizational performance: are based on the results of research done by PricewaterhouseCoopers (PWC) shown in Exhibit 8.1 on the challenges organizations face to exhibiting equitable inclusion of diverse people.[83]

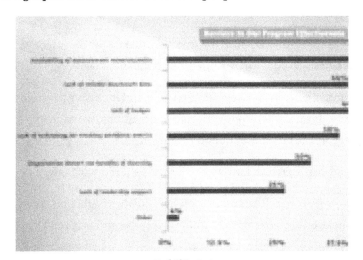

Exhibit 8.1

Here are the six barriers identified by PWC:

> **Availability of measurement resources/skills:** Angela Peacock describes how "organizations are failing to measure progress despite being all too ready to be seen to spend big and commit to all kinds of great-on-paper initiatives."[84]

➤ **Lack of reliable benchmark data:** As Nannan Hu said to me in a conversation, "It takes a lot of work to measure. And I think...sometimes organizations are afraid of what is going to turn up... once you have the data, it almost forces you to do something. I've seen passive-aggressive resistance from executives and organizations on collecting this data, because they're afraid of what they might have to do once they have the data."

➤ **Lack of budget (funding & time):** Leaders struggle constantly to secure sustainable funding for their organizations. They are unsure whether they will be able to secure additional resources to address DEI. Aside from funding, leaders also operate with limited human resources. Staff members often work long hours to fulfill the organization's mission. Leaders are unsure how they would find fiscal resources or time to engage staff members in much-needed DEI professional development.

➤ **Lack of technology for tracking workforce metrics:** Processes and systems that are not in place to track the demographics of the work force, how diverse staff are being treated, or the experiences of diverse staff.

➤ **Organization doesn't see benefits of diversity:** See the Concerns and Myths for a detailed explanation of this.

➤ **Lack of leadership support** (aka Prioritization dilution): Leaders do not make DEI a priority and/or they do not have the skills to drive organizational performance through diversity. One aspect of this is management style. Many organizations center on an "autocratic" management style. Yet autocratic management styles do not permit equitable inclusion.[85]

Additional barriers include the following.

➤ No long-range plan to integrate the values of diverse and inclusive culture with organizational objectives.

➤ Poor instructional delivery model to educate in still DEI concepts within the workforce.

➤ Lack of representation of diverse voices in the designing and leadership of the effort.[86]

Colleen Clark from Life is Good tells the story of one of the founders who asked how many man-hours were spent on the affinity group effort. She said to him, "I don't know, I don't think I can come up with a number, as I don't think we captured how many men attended which sessions." The founder was a little annoyed (for being called out for using sexist terminology) but he appreciated it in the end.

Here are even more barriers that show up in the above story (as identified by Forbes Council Member Kumar Parakala):[87]

➤ Stereotyping and unconscious bias;
➤ Tick box approach valuing only that diversity has been considered rather than equitably included;
➤ Lack of meritocracy at senior levels.

To overcome these barriers, Parakala suggests the following.

➤ Be clear about why DEI is important.
➤ Have constructive debate to encourage candid conversation and solicit actionable insights.
➤ Walk the walk, showing how to equitably included diverse people by example.
➤ Build comfort in having difficult conversations about diversity by making conversations about DEI mainstream instead of one-off conversations.
➤ Be deliberate and intentional, intervening when needed and making tough decisions.
➤ Find the right leaders to do the right things.
➤ Establish a meritocracy, not a hierarchy: ideas are more important than the hierarchy of the organization.
➤ Remember: no measurement, no improvement: improvement happens only way you measure it progress.

Challenges Once Diverse

Many organizations focus on just becoming more diverse. But just achieving diversity without equity and inclusion can be almost as bad as not working toward DEI at all as there can be negative impacts of having diversity in your organization when you have not established a culture of equitable inclusion.[88]

> ➤ Entrenchment, otherwise known as "digging in." A less strident form of rebellion and resistance is the tendency for people to associate only with people of "their own kind." Preferring segregation, they may fight efforts at integration.
>
> ➤ Miscommunication, which often can be traced to language or cultural barriers. They can be overcome, but only with time and steady, long-term commitment. Miscommunication can be frustrating, but the real cost to the owner is a reduction in workplace efficiency.
>
> ➤ Drop in morale and productivity, which often happens when employees feel disenfranchised or unhappy because there are others getting the attention they once enjoyed. It's how they make their feelings known.
>
> ➤ Unhealthy competition that pits employees against each other based on their age, gender, sexual orientation, race, religion or ethnicity – the very issues business owners are attempting to blur.
>
> ➤ Biases and stereotypes, which can be made even more complicated to remedy when you consider that people tend to conceal them, not broadcast them, and that employees often fall into a pattern of "groupthink" that can make them feel empowered.
>
> ➤ Blatant disrespect, which can breed tensions and hostilities that affect everyone in a workplace. Even people who accept and want a diverse workplace may feel frustrated and stymied.
>
> ➤ Overt conflict or retaliation, which is probably every business owner's and manager's worst nightmare.

> ➤ When animosities bubble over, verbal altercations can escalate into physical ones. But these can be handled with good management.

Key reader takeaways

Challenges to implementing a DEI program that will ignite superior organizational performance cover a wide range. Some challenges are interpersonal in nature, such as stereotyping and unconscious bias. Some challenges are operational, such as lack of technology for tracking workforce metrics. Some challenges are procedural, such as a poor instructional delivery model.

Overcoming those barriers will require significant commitment from management and leadership. It will require openness and intentionality on the part of everyone in the organization. And it will require a performance management system that holds everyone accountable for equitable inclusion of diverse people.

Consider This...

This chapter explored the challenges to implementing a DEI program toward igniting superior organizational performance.

> ➤ Does your organization's leadership understand the value of DEI?
> ➤ Does your organization's leadership exhibit equitable inclusion of diverse people?
> ➤ Is your organization relying on one person to implement your DEI efforts?
> ➤ Is the attitude in your organization that DEI should be embedded in everything you do?
> ➤ Are there measures in place to keep everyone accountable for equitable inclusion of diverse people?

Here are some questions you should ask yourself to see if you are ready to move on:

Question	Your Response
Do you understand the barriers to DEI?	
Do you understand why those barriers exist?	
Do you know how DEI impacts the three levels of Organizational Performance System?	

If you answered "yes" to these questions, then you are ready to move on to the next chapter, which looks at the signs and levers of organizational performance through diversity.

CHAPTER 9

Signs and Levers of DEI and Organizational Performance Through Diversity

---

"An organization's ability to learn, and translate that learning into action rapidly, is the ultimate competitive advantage."
—Jack Welch

Thesis: *Levels of maturity in DEI lead to understanding the levers that can be pulled on the journey to superior organizational performance.*

"Mommy, are we there yet?" Anyone who has been on a journey knows that it goes more smoothly and enjoyably when you know where you are going, have some way to know where you are, and what progress you are making.

The same is true with transformation of an organization toward superior organizational performance. Chapter 2 discussed what diversity looks like in an organization; this chapter discusses the organizational characteristics that can be used as signs of progress toward DEI. This chapter also connects DEI to organizational performance and discusses the nine levers you can pull to encourage DEI and Organizational Performance.

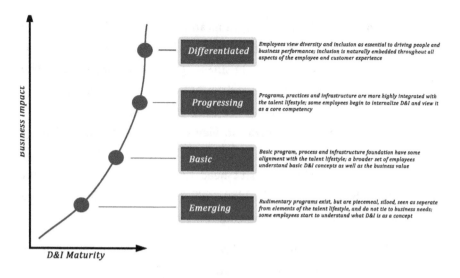

Exhibit 9.1 DEI Maturity Curve

There are characteristics (aka areas) of organizations at different levels of maturity. I think of these characteristics as signs of DEI Maturity as shown in Exhibit 9.1 DEI Maturity Curve which I created based on PWC's D&I Maturity curve. The image shows that the more mature an organization is with respect to DEI, the greater the impact is on the business/mission of the organization. (The same applies for nonprofit organizations.) Organizations at the lower levels only think about DEI tactically. if they do at all. Organizations at the higher levels think of DEI strategically. [89]

Let's examine each of the four levels:

1. **Emerging**: Rudimentary programs may exist around DEI, but they're piecemeal and are siloed—separate from the elements of the talent lifecycle (or employee lifecycle) and are not aligned to business or missional needs. Some of the employees may understand what the DEI is, as a concept; most probably do not.

2. **Basic:** Some basic DEI programs are in place. Infrastructure foundations have programs with a DEI focus and there is some alignment with a talent lifecycle. A broader set of employees understand the basic concepts of DEI, and some understand the business or missional value of DEI.

3. **Progressing:** there are programs and practices and infrastructure that are more highly integrated with the talent lifecycle and aligned to mission or business goals and objectives. The organization is starting to see the DEI as a core competency.

4. **Differentiated:** DEI is a core competency for the organization. Everyone in the organization views DEI as essential to driving business/missional performance. It is, as we say, in the DNA of the organization. There doesn't need to be a special separate DEI effort, because it is embedded and infused in everything that the organization does. It occurs naturally.

It takes time, years, to move up the levels. And some organizations never make it past the Basic level. As the creators of the Curve state:

> "Successful D&I programs all share the following main drivers: robust metrics, business-focused strategy, leadership alignment, and integrated talent processes. Companies typically don't become expert in all these areas at the same rate."[90]

They also emphasize that "A company can only ascend the D&I maturity curve when supported (and pushed) by sound data collection and analytics." Organizations that are at the lower levels relay on operational reports and surveys. They mention what they call the six "stages" of DEI data analytics:

1. basic DEI data reporting;
2. DEI surveys;
3. DEI metrics and dashboards;
4. DEI benchmarking;
5. advanced DEI analytics (e.g., gender pay equity analytics);
6. predictive DEI analytics.

Of course, implementing any of these requires having a technology capability. And you will recall (from Chapter 8) that lack of technology for tracking workforce metrics was one of the barriers to DEI.

Connecting DEI to Organizational Performance

How does DEI actually ignite superior organizational performance? To answer that question, let's look at how Howes' Organizational Performance System relates to each aspect of Organizational Performance: see Exhibit 9.2.

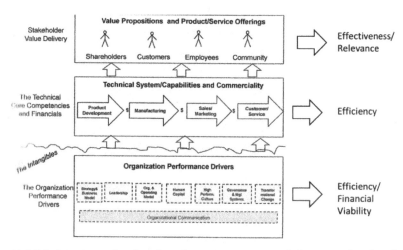

Exhibit 9.2. Organizational Performance Aspect and the Organizational Performance System

Exhibit 9.2 illustrates how the levels of the Organizational Performance System impact the aspects of Organizational Performance:

➤ Stakeholder Value Delivery describes what effect and relevance the organization will have on stakeholders, customers, employees, and community. For example, as mentioned previously, having diverse perspectives in an organization doing this work provides a better understanding of the needs of a broader set of customers and stakeholders. Thus, DEI impacts the effectiveness and relevance aspects of organizational performance.

➤ Technical Core Competencies and Financials dictates the efficiency of the organization. As mentioned previously, having diverse perspectives provides more ideas that lead to improvements in how product or service are developed, marketed, and serviced.

> ➢ Organizational Performance Drivers impact the efficiency of the organization as well as its financial viability. For example, Leadership is an Organizational Performance Driver. As mentioned previously, having diversity and the management of that diversity and the teamwork are significant predictors of organizational efficiency. Diverse perspectives provide more a better strategic business model leading to greater financial viability.

Levers of Inclusion & Organizational Performance

There are organizational levers and levers that individual leaders have.

Organizational Levers

Chapter 8 discussed one of the biggest challenges or barriers an organization faces in implementing DEI is the autocratic management styles. Management style is one of the most important levers in an organization. The most common throughout the years has been "command and control" (parent/child) management style. It is *the* management style of the military. But it is also used widely throughout corporations.

In command-and-control environments, many middle managers and most front-line employees are being told what to do, and they have learned they have no choice but to carry out their orders. Instead of pushing back or speaking their truth, most simply bite their tongues from feeling unheard at best, and unappreciated or disrespected at worst. That's not conducive to inclusion, let alone equitable inclusion.[91] Shifting to a less autocratic management style (see management style options [92]) will encourage various levels of equitable inclusion which will, in turn, improve organizational performance.

For example, the American Hospital Association has identified these levers:[93]

> ➢ Culturally appropriate patient care (or whatever product or service you provide)

➤ Equitable and inclusive organizational policies
➤ Collection and use of data to drive action
➤ Diverse representation in leadership and governance
➤ Community collaborations for solutions
➤ Systemic and shared accountability

Other levers available to the organization to encourage DEI are:[94]

➤ **Motivation:** ensuring there is assistance with and opportunities for growth and advancement that meet the different needs of each employee;
➤ **Alignment:** ensuring that organization goals and objectives align with the mission/vision that is equitable and inclusive so that employees will want to perform.
➤ **Capability:** ensuring that employees' skills are up to the tasks they have been assigned and that their diverse perspectives are useful in achieving the organization's mission.

Individual Leader Levers

Collen Clark, Head of HR at Life is Good, shared a story about a situation where there was pushback from the founders around addressing racism, after BIPoC employees asked for a statement about the George Floyd murder. The founders did not want to make a statement. They thought, "we're doing this work every day, why should be spend $25,000 to do something just to jump on the bandwagon with other brands."

However, Clark did start a discussion group when the murder took place. After a year of having the focus groups, the founders finally realized they needed to do something and said there should be discussions about this in all meetings. The fact that the Head of HR took an action is an example of the fact that individual leaders also have levers they can pull to create an inclusive environment.

Individual leaders have 10 types of motivational power:[95]

1. Legitimate
2. Coercive

3. Referent
5. Charisma
7. Information
9. Founder

4. Connection
6. Expert
8. Reward
10. Moral

They key is to know when to use which type of power. Professor Robert Livingston of Harvard University describes three types of people when it comes to DEI:

1. *Dolphins* are peace-lovers: they understand the need for DEI without you having to explain it and are ready to make it happen.
2. *Ostriches* are focused on whatever is in front of them and don't pay attention to anything else: they have their heads in the sand when it comes to DEI because it does not impact them.
3. *Sharks* are those who hold power and want to keep that status quo of them being in control: they see DEI as a threat to their power and control.[96]

You don't have to do anything to motivate the dolphins to move toward DEI. The Ostriches need a "carrot" to motivate them toward DEI. The Sharks need a stick to force them toward DEI. Leaders trying to implement DEI must understand with which type of person they are dealing and choose the appropriate motivational power.

Chapter 10 discusses what leaders can do through policies and procedures to equitably include diverse people.

Key reader takeaways

There are many characteristics that indicate signs of progress toward DEI and organizational performance. They are well-described in the PwC DEI Maturity Curve. The curve shows increasing maturity in DEI starting at the Emerging level where DEI is, if at all addressed, addressed by a few individuals in the organization to the Differentiated level where DEI is embedded in everything the organization does.

DEI ignites superior organizational performance through improving the organizational performance system. Levers that can be pulled toward DEI are significantly influenced by management style. Autocratic management styles do not lend themselves to DEI. More permissive management styles allow for and encourage different levels of inclusion.

Consider This...

This chapter explored the signs and levers of organizational performance:

➢ Where is your organization on the DEI Maturity curve?
➢ Is your leadership style conducive to DEI?
➢ To what levers do you have access that could increase DEI?

This chapter described signs of progress toward DEI and levers that can be used to move up increase equitable inclusion of diverse people. Here are some questions you should ask yourself to see if you are ready to move on:

Question	Your Response
Do you understand the characteristics of organizational performance at the various levels of DEI maturity?	
Do you understand how DEI ignites organizational performance?	
Do you understand the impact management style has on DEI?	
Do you know the types of levers that can be pulled to encourage DEI?	

If you answered "yes" to these questions, then you are ready to move on to the next chapter, which discusses the actual journey an organization should take toward organizational performance through diversity.

The Roadmap to Organizational Performance

"Creating and managing a diverse workforce is a process,
not a destination."
—R. Roosevelt Thomas, Jr.

Thesis: *Achieving certain milestones will ignite organizational performance.*

Now that we understand what diversity is, that it is nothing without equitable inclusion of diverse people; we understand why DEI does not exist; what it actually looks like; what the challenges or barriers are to achieving it; what signs indicate we are moving toward fully embracing DEI; and what levers can be pulled to leverage it, let us now look at a roadmap to organizational performance through diversity.

Igniting superior performance through diversity is a change management initiative with the goal of improving organizational performance. There are many change management methodologies, from the well-known Prosci Methodology to the Viral Change Roadmap. But they are not specific to DEI.

There are several models for implementing DEI from livingHR's DEI Transformation Model to CultureSync's four-phased approach. But they do not seem to tie directly to organizational performance.

All of these methodologies and models have steps that are common. They all seem to follow Deming's Plan-Do-Check-Act (PDCA) cycle for continuous improvement, shown in Exhibit 10.1.

Exhibit 10.1. Plan-Do-Check-Act Continuous Improvement Cycle[97]

The Discovering Performance Through Diversity Roadmap I have developed combines the best of these two types of methodologies. It also incorporates the positive steps for leaders to create sustainable change (according to John P. Kotter[98]) as discussed in Chapter 7 in the section on Organizational Performance Drivers. It also incorporates what I call the five milestones to DEI, shown in Exhibit 10.2, and combines them into one master Transformation Plan.

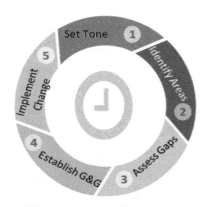

Exhibit 10.2. Five Milestones to DEI

Let's look at this Roadmap in a little more detail.

Plan

Planning is a critical starting point for any DEI effort—or, for that matter, any effort that impacts a number of people in an organization. It involves:

- ➢ understanding the current state of the organization;
- ➢ understanding where the organization could go;
- ➢ understanding what could be done given the organization's resources to get it where it should be;
- ➢ defining at a high-level how the organization will move the effort forward.

Do

Doing the work of the high-level plan that will implementing the change toward superior organization performance involves:

- ➢ adding detail to the existing Action Plan;
- ➢ updating and implementing policies and procedures; and
- ➢ training staff on how to execute those policies and procedures.

Check

Checking progress involves monitoring and controlling the work being done. Regular progress reports should be made according to the governance process identified during the Plan phase.

Act/Adjust

Acting/adjusting involves reflecting on the progress made in the execution of the Action Plan and making adjustments to the overall approach to DEI. This is input for a new Plan phase.

Continuous Improvement

The PDCA cycle should not be executed just once. You will recall that Chapter 9: Signs and Levers of DEI and Organizational Performance Through Diversity described that every organization is on a journey. That journey starts somewhere on PwC's DEI Maturity Curve – wherever your organization may be. The cycle should repeat over and over again (and it may take years) for as long as the organization exists to move it up the curve.

Here is an example of a journey a company could take maturing in DEI. If your organization starts at the Emerging level, you go through the PDCA cycle and (hopefully), you will have matured to the Basic level. You go through the cycle again; once through it (hopefully), you will have matured to the Progressing level. You go through the cycle again: this time, you are still at the Progressing level. You go through the cycle again, and again, and again, and you are still at the Progressing level. Some organizations never get to Differentiated. Remember, this could—and will probably—be years after you first started your DEI efforts.

Key reader takeaways

The Discovering Performance Through Diversity Roadmap is based on the well-known Deming Plan-Do-Check-Act (PDCA) model. The PDCA model represents a cycle. So, the Roadmap is a cycle.

The Roadmap looks at the three levels of Howes' Organizational Performance System. The Roadmap can and probably should be repeated as long as the organization exists to make the organization more mature in its leveraging DEI and move up the PwC Maturity Curve. As the organization moves up the curve, performance should increase.

Consider This...

This chapter defined the Roadmap to organizational performance through diversity.

- ➢ How does your organization handle cross-functional efforts?
- ➢ How successful cross-functional efforts are in your organization?
- ➢ What challenges or resistance can you envision to this work in your organization?
- ➢ What levers could be pulled in each of the Roadmap phases?

This DEI Roadmap provides a framework and set of steps for igniting superior organizational performance. Here are some questions you should ask yourself to see if you are ready to move on:

Question	Your Response
Do you understand the phases of the DEI Roadmap?	
Do you understand the importance of planning your DEI effort?	

If you answered "yes" to these questions, then you're ready to move on to the next chapter, which discusses the planning phase of the journey.

PART 5

Beginning the Journey to Igniting Organizational Performance Through Diversity

Set the tone and framework; Create Initial Program Schedule; Establish Goals and Governance; and Perform a Current State Analysis to plan for a smooth journey.

CHAPTER 11

Set the Tone and Framework

"Without leaps of imagination, or dreaming, we lose the excitement of possibilities. Dreaming, after all, is a form of planning."
—Gloria Steinem

Thesis: *Planning is what allows you to see all the pieces of a DEI effort and how to orchestrate them toward superior organizational performance.*

The imperatives for successfully achieving superior organizational performance through diversity are summarized by McKinsey's January 18, 2018 report "Delivering through diversity" Imperatives to deliver inclusive growth.

➢ Articulate and cascade CEO commitment to galvanize the organization. Companies increasingly recognize that commitment to inclusion and diversity starts at the top, with many companies publicly committing to an I&D agenda.

➢ Define inclusion and diversity priorities that are based on the drivers of the business-growth strategy.

> ➤ Craft a targeted portfolio of inclusion and diversity initiatives to transform the organization.
> ➤ Tailor the strategy to maximize local impact.

Planning sets the context for all of the work done in the Operational Performance System's levels of Technical Core Competencies and Finances and Organizational Performance Drivers. Let's look at each of the steps of the Planning phase that implement McKinsey's imperatives.

Step 1: Set the Tone

It is important to set the tone for any program to succeed. Without setting the tone, people will not prioritize the effort and will have an attitude they choose rather that the attitude necessary to ignite superior organizational performance. Setting the tone has to do with attitude and structure.

The tone being set is that everyone will always use an equity lens. Chapter 4: What Is This Term "Diversity"? provided a formula for what makes a welcoming /inclusive/high-performing organization: Equitable inclusion of diverse people.

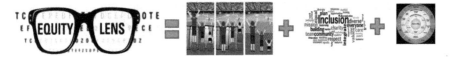

Exhibit 11.1. Equity Lens

That same formula can be used to the tone to be set as using an equity lens. Everyone in the organization will equitably include diverse people.

Truly setting the tone for a DEI effort includes the following steps (all discussed in the remainder of this chapter):

> ➤ painting a picture of what success looks like so everyone knows where they are heading;
> ➤ establishing cultural norms and principles so that there are guidelines for the expected new behaviors

➢ making DEI a priority so that everyone knows to put an emphasis on it;

➢ acknowledging that embracing DEI will take time as it involves a cultural change and that cultures changes slowly so the expectation is set that that this is a long-term journey.

Step 2: Paint a Picture of Success

We should keep in mind what we are striving for, what success looks like. As Attorney Nick Holmes of Devine Millimet, shared with me, we know we have been successful "when race, sex, age is not a consideration for filling a position and there are frequent conversations about issues of discrimination."

Painting a picture of success for a DEI effort includes creating a DEI vision statement and communicating that statement. The statement should connect DEI with the organization's strategic goals.

From a communications standpoint, the statement should come from the Board of the organization so everyone knows the organization takes the issue very seriously. The statement should be communicated as widely as possible using as many communications channels as possible. This includes, but is not limited to company newsletters, website, social media, annual reports, etc.

Step 3: Establish Cultural Norms and Principles

Organizational culture and norms are based on values and principles, as shown in Exhibit 11.3.

Values are qualities or standards of behavior. They are beliefs and opinions that an organization holds dear. Examples of DEI-related values include:

➢ Respect

➢ Fairness

➢ Dignity

➢ Inclusion

- ➤ Equity
- ➤ Adapting
- ➤ Diversity
- ➤ Welcome

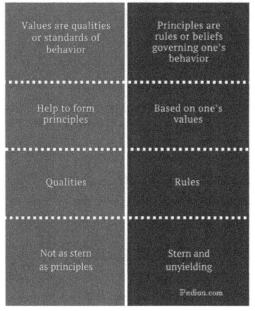

Exhibit 11.3. Difference Between Values and Principles[99]

Principles are rules or beliefs governing a person's behavior. They provide the guideposts for the behavior we want to see. Examples of DEI-related principles include:

- ➤ Promote a culture of respect, support, and inclusion;
- ➤ Further educate ourselves and engage our community in actions to promote Diversity, Equity and Inclusion
- ➤ Remove barriers towards equal opportunities in the way we advertise and recruit for our roles
- ➤ Have a zero-tolerance policy for demeaning language or behavior based on race, gender, age, disability.
- ➤ Provide equal pay to our employees regardless of gender identity and/or expression.

Step 4: Make DEI a Priority

One executive with whom I spoke said that "If every last one of your managers and team leaders cannot make a clear, granular business case for creating an inclusive environment, you need to get to the point where they can." So, they can push for everyone to make DEI a priority.

Senior leader sponsorship of a DEI effort is important to its success. Curt Howes told me that "You need sponsor acceptance, though, to make diverse ideas come about."

Armando Llorente shared the story of a large manufacturing organization with facilities around the east coast. A new VP of HR was a visionary who replaced the previous VP, who had worked for the company for 30 years. The new VP held an event with the team leadership, leaders went back to their plants, and that was it: the VP never called the group together or followed up. Because of the lack of follow-up, leadership questioned whether this was a real initiative.

This tone can and should apply to dealing with partners or suppliers as well. Nick Holmes of Devine Millimet shared that a major construction company had a well-popularized DEI plan. But the company decided it needed to take more action. The company created a policy of pushing DEI Plan requirements on their subcontractors. On a major construction project, managers heard that graffiti was being written on the building. They stopped the construction and did awareness training. After the training, workers thanked the company for the effort. The amount of harassment lowered and the project was completed early.

Step 5: Acknowledge the Long-Term Journey

There should be a shared recognition that accomplishing DEI will take time. As Nick Holmes of Devine Millimet shared, "Progress is made one conversation at a time, one decision at a time. Having a goal is not enough. You have to work on it every time you have a conversation."

Nick also shared that companies should not "take your foot off the gas pedal. You're not going to solve this in one year. You have to be patient and keep at it. I've seen this in law firms where a statement is made and they think that's it– they never get back to the issue. We all need to be patient and accept the stumbles we make."

Consider a change of organizational structure to make sure the organization keeps at the effort for the long-term. Setting the tone is also about structuring our organizations to send the right signals and encourage the right behaviors. Frederick Laloux describes the evolution of organizations from a top-down approach to one that grows the full potential of each person and allows much greater autonomy and peer-to-peer collaboration.[100]

So how do we follow this advice and these imperatives? We start by identifying and analyzing areas where DEI is lacking This is the start of work that needs to be coordinated. So, we need to create an initial DEI program schedule to properly execute and track the work.

Step 6: Create an Initial Program Schedule

Creating an initial program schedule for igniting superior performance through diversity involves the discipline of Program/Project Management. It ensures everyone knows the steps necessary to close the gaps which will help achieve the goals identified toward the vision articulated.

At this point, the planning that should take place should generate a schedule for:

- ➢ Stakeholder Analysis[101];
- ➢ Identifying goals and governance;
- ➢ Identifying who will drive the DEI effort.

The detail scheduling of moving the organization toward those goals will come in the DO phase.

Key reader takeaways

Planning for igniting superior organizational performance takes time. It requires the Board and senior leadership setting the tone for the effort. This is done through creating and communicating a vision of how the organization should move toward the Differentiated DEI maturity level and making it clear that this effort is it a priority for the long-term.

Planning also includes identifying the steps that will be taken to achieving the vision. Professional Program Management is required for the success of this type of effort.

Consider This...

This chapter explored setting the tone and framework for your organization to exhibit equitable inclusion of diverse people.

> ➢ Does your organization have a vision for DEI?
> ➢ What cultural norms exist in your organization?
> ➢ Are your organization values and principles aligned with diversity, equity, and inclusion?
> ➢ What priority has your organization put on DEI?

This chapter described the planning phase of the Organizational Performance Through Diversity Roadmap. Here are some questions you should ask yourself to see if you are ready to move on:

Question	Your Response
Do you understand how to set the tone for igniting superior organizational performance?	
Do you understand the difference between values and principles?	
Do you understand how to make DEI a priority?	

If you answered "yes" to these questions, then you're ready to move on to the next chapter, which discusses establishing goals and governance for the DEI effort.

CHAPTER 12

Establish Goals and Governance

"The bottom line is, when people are crystal clear about the most important priorities of the organization and team they work with and prioritized their work around those top priorities, not only are they many times more productive, they discover they have the time they need to have a whole life"
—Stephen Covey

Thesis: *Setting DEI goals and metrics requires thinking about how DEI impacts the organizational performance system.*

With the analysis of where gaps exist complete, let's look at establishing DEI-specific goals and establishing the governance of a DEI effort.

Goals

DEI goals are the target for everyone in the organization to reach for. DEI Goals that support and align with organizational goals help the organization focus on work that will eliminate Fear Ignorance Uncertainty and Doubt (FIUD) and motivate equitable inclusion of diverse people.

Remember, we mentioned that Angela Peacock makes the observation, "...organizations are failing to measure progress despite being all too ready to be seen to spend big and commit to all kinds of great-on-paper initiatives."

"Our goal is to establish language that is gender-neutral, ethnic-neutral and age-neutral, while celebrating our spirit of diversity."

The impact of setting DEI goals is proven and powerful. Brie Elliot of Ballentine Partners shared that they established a goal to be >50% female. They are now at 54% and have noticed improved employee satisfaction.

The following questions can be a guide to determining DEI goals and the impact of DEI on the organization:

> How does DEI contribute to delivery of organization performance goals (effectiveness/relevance)?

> How are DEI considerations incorporated into decisions on key topics such as members, services, and location (efficiency)?

> How are leaders held accountable for DEI results (Effectiveness)?

> What mechanisms are in place to monitor and respond to what is working - and what is not? (Efficiency/Financial Viability)

> How effectively do programs create a more inclusive environment, and not only a more diverse one? (effectiveness)

Setting goals takes time. The effort should be planned just as any other part of the effort should be planned. This section explores the various types of DEI goals that could be stablished, metrics that can be used to track progress toward those goals, and how organizational governance should ensure those goals are met. Keep in mind, there are some legal considerations when identifying goals. Laws around quotas are complex and can differ from state to state. The general advice seems to be set goals, not quotas.[102]

Types of Goals and Metrics

Goals should be designed around the three organizational performance system levels. They should be developed following guidance shared by Frank Dobbin and Alexandra:

> "A number of companies have gotten consistently positive results with tactics that don't focus on control. They apply three basic principles: engage managers in solving the problem, expose them to people from different groups, and encourage social accountability for change."[103]

When establishing goals, one should always keep in mind the DEI vision previously established as well as the cultural aspects identified in setting the tone step as described in Chapter 11.

Metrics are needed to help ensure progress is being made toward goals. They can be thought of as Key Performance Indicators (KPIs). Aura Huot of Lavalee Brensinger Architects makes the point that organizations "need to assess performance. [For example] Is collaboration happening? When organizations are not using KPIs, they miss the boat. They don't know if efforts are working or not working."

Consider the story of Atos as shared with me by Chief Diversity Officer Denise Lamoreaux. Atos is a tech company that decided it wanted to work toward "techquity" by assessing the number of women in the company, trying to get metrics with respect to people of color, age, and disabilities. The leaders emphasized engagement of key people (e.g., via mentoring, talent program participation, ability to expand.)

They examine what happens once people of color are "in the door," making sure they have opportunities available to grow. With this approach, their biggest success story is growth in women in leadership from 13% to 30% in one year.

They have a strong focus on generational metrics, trying to track the percentage of employees from different age brackets because they want to be prepared from a succession progression and knowledge transfer perspective for those who are looking to retire. They also want to make sure that they don't have just one particular generation making up a majority of the workforce, because they want that diversity of thought that comes from the different generational perspectives.

They look at the percentage of people with disabilities who are working within the organization to harness the energy that comes from the way they look at problems and solutions.

One of the other key areas they're always looking at is the engagement of their key people. Are they involved in mentoring others? Are they involved in able to participate in talent programs? Are they getting an opportunity to grow?

Not only do they look at representation, but they also look at the impact diversity has on effectiveness. They look at the diversity makeup of sales teams to see whether they consist of mostly men or if there is a mix of gender, generations, ethnicities, and/or races.

As Nannan Hu said,

> "As the age-old saying goes, you can't improve what you can't measure, right? So, if you're really committed to improving DEI, the first step is how do you measure it? In our all-hands meetings, whether they be monthly or quarterly, we always dedicate a section of that to discuss our DEI metrics. And in terms of what we measured, it was not only the most basic things—like what is the composition of the employees; what percentage are from what group; what percentage are male, female, non-binary—but we also looked at it particularly in management. So, if x percent of your employee base is of a certain group, is that represented in

the management level? And what we found was that while we did really well, in terms of an overall kind of mix of diverse employees, when it came to management, we still had the same issues and tendencies as any other company, which was we skewed male, and we skewed white."

Curt Howes identified a goal area not usually thought of during a recent discussion we had. He indicated that there should be metrics around succession planning.

Identifying Goals & Metrics

A DEI Goals Framework I developed that is helpful in identifying goals describes 19 areas divided into 4 categories: Business/Mission, People, Process, and Facilities/Technology based on my own work and work described in a number of sources.[104][105][106][107]

Keep in mind that a goal is a direction in which you want to go. A metric is a measurement indicating whether that goal has been achieved. Each goal should have at least one metric and is ideally a "SMART" goal (Specific, Measurable, Assignable, Realistic, and Time-related).[108]

Business/Mission

DEI goals around *business/mission* relate to the Stakeholder Value Delivery and the Operational Performance Drivers (except for Human Capital) level of Howes' Organizational Performance System. The areas in this category are shown in Exhibit 12.1.

Business			
Positive PR (vs. Negative PR)	Legal	Market Penetration/Share	Customer Satisfaction

Exhibit 12.1. Business/Mission Goals

Goals could be developed in the following areas:

➤ **Public Relations**: the number of positive press coverage, awards, or press releases related to DEI over the year;

➤ **Legal**: whether the number of discrimination lawsuits in a year is fewer than the previous year;

➤ **Market Penetration/Share (or in a non-profit parlance, Served Penetration)**: market share or those served should represent the demographics of the area in which we serve;

➤ **Customer Satisfaction**: customer satisfaction ratings (you are performing customer surveys, aren't you?).

Each of these areas has an impact on organizational effectiveness.

People

DEI goals around *people* relate to the Human Capital driver of the Organizational Performance Drivers level of Howes' Organizational Performance System. They ensure there is a focus on monitored groups (people with dimensions of their personality we want to include). The areas in this category are shown in Exhibit 12.2.

People			
Representation Metrics	Recruitment Metrics	Staffing/Placement Metrics	Transaction Metrics
Training Metrics	Workplace Climate Metrics	Retention Metrics	Employee Satisfaction Metrics

Exhibit 12.2. People Goals

Goals could be developed in the following areas:

➤ **Representation Metrics**: Comparing representation of monitored groups to an identified internal or external benchmark;

➢ **Recruitment Metrics**: Compare representation of monitored groups in the applicant pool to an identified benchmark;

➢ **Staffing/Placement Metrics**: Compare representation of monitored groups hired or placed to an identified benchmark;

➢ **Transaction Metrics:** Are monitored groups being retained, advanced, etc. at "expected" rates relative to benchmark?

➢ **Training Metrics**: Evaluate penetration of diversity-related training, general training participation rates, and demographics of talent pipeline;

➢ **Workplace Climate Metrics**: Using trend analysis of workplace climate survey results to compare of organizational units to broader company benchmarks;

➢ **Retention Metrics**: Establishing an attrition rate target for a certain class of people;

➢ **Employee Satisfaction**: Not only how satisfied employees are with their work but tied to customer satisfaction.

Aura Huot of Brensinger Architects shared: "Another metric that I think is very important in terms of DE&I is...learning and development in general. Tracking your training. If you don't know what type of training you are providing, what type of coaching you're providing, and how that is impacting the organization, we as an organization are missing the boat."

Exhibit 12.3 provides some examples, based on an article by renowned training metrics thought leaders Jim Kirkpatrick and Wendy Kirkpatrick.[109]

Exhibit 12.3. Example Goals for Diversity, Equity, and Inclusion

Diversity	Equity	Inclusion
➢ % of diverse candidates who apply, interview, or are hired for a position ➢ % of diverse employees at each level	➢ Salary parity for diverse employees at the same level⁺ ➢ Equal opportunities available for all employees	➢ All voices heard equally during committee meetings ➢ Frequency and types of opportunities for employees to

➢ Diversity of employees promoted to higher levels or Advanced Physicians ➢ % Retention of diverse employees ➢ Increase in Employee Engagement among diverse workers ➢ Increase in diversity of executive board members	➢ Equitable Performance Management and succession planning practices ➢ # of trainings diversity, equity and inclusion in in the next year.	provide input on decisions that affect them directly ➢ Positive employee survey results on questions related to feeling respected and valued for their country ➢ Developing communication systems that connect front-line employees to top-level leaders ➢ Building organizational capacity for behaviors that foster psychological safety

+ An example of potentially a problematic promotion policy used by many companies involves limiting the number of promotions that can occur in a year. This type of policy is usually put into place to save money. However, this can be seen as discriminatory by someone of an underrepresented class whose performance was stellar, yet they did not receive a promotion when a White male with the same performance rating was promoted.

The same situation can occur where managers have a certain "pot" of money to reward their reports and divide that pot any way they want. Someone from an underrepresented class who receives less of a raise than a White male with the same performance rating will see this as discrimination by the manager or the company.

Benchmarks for these goals can be taken from the following sources:

➢ The U.S. Bureau of Labor Statistics

- ➤ The <u>U.S. Census Bureau</u>
- ➤ World Bank <u>Open Data</u>
- ➤ Organisation for Economic Co-Operation and Development (<u>OECD</u>)
- ➤ Associations in your industry

For example, the U.S. Census Bureau can be used as the basis for a goal around the percentage of diverse candidates who apply, interview, or are hired for a position. The goal might be that the number of candidates who apply for a position should reflect the demographics of the community in which the organization operates.

Each of these areas has an impact on organizational efficiency and relevance.

Process

DEI goals around *process* relate to the Human Capital driver of the Organizational Performance Drivers level of Howes' Organizational Performance System. The areas in this category are shown in Exhibit 12.4.

Exhibit 12.4 Process Goals

An example impact of process goals comes from Armando Llorente. Metrics on innovation are very helpful as one company with whom he worked established "quarterly MBOs that were reviewed, such as team effectiveness, career pathing, quality, profitability. Focus on change in metrics was on staffing. They tracked the change of the staff demographics. They tracked what ideas were identified to solve problems."

Goals could be developed in the following areas:

➤ **Ideation/Innovation:** the number of ideas generated by women is 10% greater than last year;

➤ **Supplier Diversity:** all suppliers will provide a DEI plan by the end of the year;

➤ **Decision-making:** all major decisions will have considered at least one idea from a woman.

Each of these areas has an impact on organizational efficiency and financial viability.

Facilities/Technology

DEI goals around *facilities and technology* relate to the aspects of the Organization & Operating Model and the Government's Management Systems drivers of the organization performance drivers level of Howes' Organizational Performance System. The areas in this category are shown in Exhibit 12.5.

Technology			
Environmental Impact	Building Accessibility	Computer Accessibility (Section 508)	Diversity Data

Exhibit 12.5. Facilities/Technology Goals

An example impact of Facilities/Technology goals is the Interstate-91 expansion project in Worchester, MA. The expansion was built on top of lands previously inhabited by people of color. The city took their land by eminent domain rather than routing it through less dense land just around it.

Goals could be developed in the following areas:

➤ **Environmental Impact:** decisions will not be made that have environmental ramifications that negatively impact those least able to mitigate the dangers caused by that decision;

- ➤ **Building Accessibility:** 50% of the doors (whether or not we own the building) will be wheelchair accessible;
- ➤ **Computer Accessibility:** by the end of the year, all software and computers will comply with Section 508 of the Rehabilitation Act of 1973.[110]

Each of these areas has an impact on organizational efficiency and relevance.

Governance

Chapter 1 discussed the research from McKinsey and others that proves that organizations that are diverse and have diversity in their leadership are more likely to outperform their peers.

The organization's Board is responsible for ensuring organizational performance. Thus, it is critical for the Board to understand that diversity, equity, and inclusion will help them achieve organizational performance.

Once the Board understands that, there are several actions it needs to take:

- ➤ Make a public statement about how the organization values DEI.
- ➤ Provide DEI training to all Board members.
- ➤ Ensure that the Board membership is diverse. Board members themselves must be willing to reach into groups of people that they're not accustomed to reaching into. The "old boy" or "old buddy" network does not necessarily work for this.
- ➤ Chapter 11: Set the Tone and Framework mentioned that the organization's Board needs to establish DEI as an organizational priority to show that the organization feels it is important enough for the Board to make a statement.
- ➤ Take a Board DEI Assessment.
- ➤ Identify someone on the Board whose responsibility it is to keep up with the DEI efforts in the organization.

> ➢ Schedule time during each Board meeting for a report from the leadership on how the DEI efforts are going. This will make the Board's commitment to DEI concretely evident.

At this point, a senior leader should be identified to lead the DEI effort so that his or her actions will be respected and his or her request will be given priority.

Key reader takeaways

DEI goals must be established to ensure the organization achieves the benefits of DEI. Those goals should be SMART and address the four categories of business/mission, people, process, and facilities/technology.

Corporate Governance is driven by the Board. The Board must ensure that the Board itself and the entire organization is structured and operates with equitable inclusion of diverse people.

Consider This...

This chapter explored establishing goals and the governance structure for exhibiting equitable inclusion of diverse people.

> ➢ Do you know how diverse your organization is currently?
> ➢ Do you know the number of ideas that were generated by diverse people over the last year?
> ➢ Do you know how many new innovations came from those ideas?
> ➢ Does your organization have goals that address the four categories?

How many of the 19 goal areas does your organization address?

This chapter described establishing goals and the governance structure portion of the Planning phase. Here are some questions you should ask yourself to see if you are ready to move on:

Question	Your Response
Do you understand the different types of DEI goals?	
Do you understand why it is so important for the Board to take the lead in a DEI effort?	
Do you understand the role of Corporate Governance in a DEI effort?	

If you answered "yes" to these questions, then you're ready to move on to the next chapter, which discusses the Do phase – making changes that will achieve the goals identified in the Plan phase.

PART 6

Igniting Superior Organizational Performance Though Diversity

Implementation of DEI involves the Do, Check, Act/Adjust Phases of the roadmap.

CHAPTER 13

Do - Current State Analysis

"You have to know who you are, if you don't you have nightmares."
—Stephen Rea

Thesis: *Performing a current state analysis is critical to knowing what needs to be changed.*

The Do phase includes the following.

➢ Updating the program schedule – identifying actions
➢ Identifying areas for investigation

> ➤ Assessing gaps
> ➤ Designing change toward DEI
> ➤ Scheduling and implementation

This chapter discusses the first part of the Do phase: updating the program schedule, identifying areas, and assessing gaps.

Update Program Schedule – Identifying Actions

At this point, the original Program Schedule should be fleshed out more to determine changes to be made. This should be performed by someone skilled in discipline of Program/Project Management. This will ensure everyone knows the steps necessary to close the gaps which will help achieve the goals identified toward the vision articulated. Or as I like to say, the "Action Plan" describes *people* using *technology and facilities* to perform work *processes* to accomplish the organization's *business/mission.*

In project management parlance, this effort is a program that will contain multiple projects/initiatives. For example, there will likely be a project and to analyze policies and procedures. There will likely be a separate project to develop training on DEI. These projects will likely have their own Planning/Scheduling phases. All these projects together will help ignite superior organizational performance.

At this point, a sample Program Schedule might look something like Exhibit 13.1.

Exhibit 13.1. Sample Program Schedule—Identifying Actions

Task	Who	Completion Date
Identify Areas to Analyze	DEI Program Manager	XX-XXX-XXXX
Analyze Gaps	TBD	XX-XXX-XXXX
Implement Changes	TBD	XX-XXX-XXXX

At this point you should also:

> ➢ establish project standards and written templates for documentation and planning;
> ➢ select project planning tools, such as Microsoft Project or Slack.

Identify Areas

Identifying areas to be addressed involves getting a lay of the land with respect to DEI. The areas to be investigated are described in the 3 levels of Howes' Organizational Performance System discussed in Chapter 7.

You should identify the structures and groups in your organization that map to the structures and groups described in the Organizational Performance System. For example, some organizations call the Product Development group the "R&D Group." This will make the next step—the assessment step—more applicable to your organization.

Assess Gaps

Assessing gaps in understanding or leveraging diversity helps us determine where the organization is with respect to DEI and what needs to be done to improve toward the vision of DEI previously articulated.

Chapter 12 discussed the goals and metrics to be measured. Next, we must determine what questions we will ask related to those metrics and how we will gather the data to answer those questions.

Questions to Ask

To assess the gaps, we gather data to try to answer the following high-level questions (they should look familiar as we saw them when we talked about DEI principles):

> ➢ How does DEI contribute to delivery of organization performance goals (effectiveness/relevance)?

➤ How are DEI considerations incorporated into decisions on key topics such as members, services, and location (efficiency)?

➤ How are leaders held accountable for DEI results (Effectiveness)?

➤ What mechanisms are in place to monitor and respond to what is working - and what is not? (Efficiency/Financial Viability)

➤ How effectively do programs create a more inclusive environment, and not only a more diverse one? (effectiveness)

Here is how I think about breaking down the questions above to analyze the organizational performance areas at each level.

Stakeholder Value Delivery (Business/Mission)

At the Stakeholder Value Delivery level, we look at the value proposition of our products/services ask questions such as:

➤ Did our Industry Trend Analysis involve as many diverse perspectives as possible so as to better able to understand a wide variety of trends occurring in the world our products/services will play?

➤ Are our stakeholders as diverse as they could be?

➤ Do our products and/or services provide value to a diverse group of customers/clients?

If the answer is "no" or "somewhat" to any of these questions, then this provides some insights into what should be done at the subsequent levels.

Technical Core Competencies and Financials

At the Technical Core Competencies and Financials level, we look at the organization's fundamentals.[111]

Bizmanualz identified 10 core business processes[112] in every organization, as shown in Exhibit 13.2.

We can look at how the equity lens is being used in each of the 10 core processes as a starting point. These map to the elements in the Technical Core Competencies & Financials.

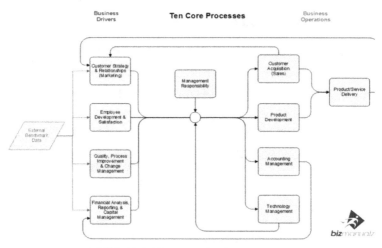

Exhibit 13.2. Ten Core Business Processes

Your organization may have other processes as well. They should also be included in your analysis.

Questions to ask include:

> ➤ Are technical requirements for the business defined in such a way as not to be discriminatory?
> ➤ Are the technical work processes for selling, developing, and delivering products and services sensitive to the needs of diverse audiences?
> ➤ Have you incorporated explicit DEI steps in all 10 top core business processes?
> ➤ Do key performance requirements for products or services include those that would apply to diverse audiences?
> ➤ Are IT and facilities sensitized to implicit bias?

If the answer is "no" or "somewhat" to either of these questions, then this provides some insights into what should be done at the subsequent levels.

Organization Performance Drivers

DEI has an impact on each organizational performance driver. This section explores the impact on each driver.

Strategic & Business Model

Using Porter's Five Forces[113] model (shown again in Exhibit 7.2) allows us to think about how DEI plays into the organization's business/mission. Exhibit 13.4 describes the impact of DEI on each of the five forces.

Exhibit 13.3. Impact of DEI on Porter's Five Forces

Threat	Impact of DEI/Questions to ask
Threats of new entrants	No impact.
Bargaining power of suppliers	Suppliers are starting to want to work with customers who have a DEI strategy. Do you have a DEI strategy for how to deal with suppliers? How diverse are your suppliers?
Bargaining power of customers	Customers are starting to want to work with customers who have a DEI strategy. Does your product/service project support of DEI?
Competitive Rivalry	Your competition may be more involved in the customer community and better equipped to address the diverse needs of a broad range of customers/clients. How does your product/service support diverse audiences as compared to your competition?
Threat of substitutes	No impact.

Some questions to ask that may help answer our original questions are related to the seven core subjects social responsibility espoused in ISO 26,000 Guidance on Social Responsibility[114]:

1. **Human rights:** Does your organization sell to or anyone regardless of any personality characteristics on the Diversity Wheel?
2. **Labor:** See the section on Human Capital (later in this chapter) for these questions.

3. **Environment**: Is your organization doing development with a sensitivity to areas of living for distressed populations?
4. **Fair operating:** Are you buying from diverse suppliers or suppliers with DEI programs?
5. **Consumer**: Are your products and/or support provided in all the languages that are primary for your customers? Do you sell your product in locations convenient for diverse customers? For example, if you make band-aids, are they colored to match the various skin tones of people of color?
6. **Organizational Governance**: See the section on Governance & Management Systems (later in this chapter) for these questions.
7. **Community Involvement:** Are there people in your organization who look like or relate to the community and help improve it?

Leadership

Leaders should use the policies and procedures (especially when decision-making processes to increase innovation), talent life cycle, the concept of high-performance teams, and balanced scorecard framework to ignite organizational performance through diversity).

Brie Elliott, VP of HR of Ballentine Partners councils to "make sure your leadership (C-Suite) team is not just giving lip service to DEI."

Questions to ask about this area include:

➢ Is the leader of the DEI program a senior person in the company so that his or her actions will be respected and his or her request will be given priority?
➢ Are leaders in the organization trained on how to be good leaders and not just promoted to management and expected to perform because they have years of experience doing the work of their group?
➢ Are leaders held accountable for DEI?
➢ Is there a decision-making model used by the organization that ensures surfacing and inclusion of ideas from diverse people?

Organization & Operating Model

Remembering that the organization and operating model defines key roles and core functions, we can look at organizational structure. The four functional designs to be considered (as shown in Exhibit 13.4), are:[115]

> ➤ Product-focused
> ➤ Functional-focused
> ➤ Customer-focused
> ➤ Geographical-focused
> ➤ Matrix/Process owners

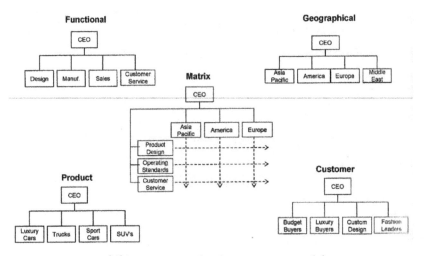

Exhibit 13.4. Organization Structure models

Of course, each model has its pros and cons. Questions to ask include:

> ➤ Are the key positions required for the structure described in ways that would not preclude the attraction or hiring of diverse people?
> ➤ Are the key responsibilities for various roles described in ways that would not hinder but actually enhance the performance of diverse people?

Human Capital

Remembering the HR Talent Life-Cycle, questions to ask include:

➤ Do you provide recurring training on implicit bias, cultural competency, and communications between diverse people?

➤ Do your recruitment policies and procedures explicitly account for implicit bias?

➤ Do your hiring policies and procedures explicitly account for implicit bias?

➤ Do your career development opportunities, assistance, policies and procedures explicitly account for implicit bias?

➤ How many cases of discrimination reported internally over the past year by race, gender, age, ethnicity, ability?

➤ How many discrimination complaints have been filed against the organization?

➤ Are staff satisfaction ratings for staff of different ages, races, genders, abilities, and thinking styles the same as staff satisfaction for white males in your organization?

➤ Are career development opportunities sensitized to the needs of diverse employees?

➤ Are awards and recognition sensitize to what motivates diverse employees?

➤ Is there pay equity between white males and diverse staff?

➤ Are coaching and mentoring opportunities provided through people who have the same background and experiences?

High-Performing Culture

As mentioned, a high-performing culture begets high-performing teams. Questions to ask include:

➤ Do processes and systems align with or support the values and principles of DEI to create a culture of inclusiveness and equity?

➤ Is culture measured, continually reinforced, and shaped?

➤ Do all teams exhibit the characteristics described in the PWC high-performing teams model?

Governance and Management Systems

Governance and Management Systems are designed to ensure the organization operates according to plan. Based on change management research,[116] questions to ask include:

- ➢ Are there people in your organization's Board and leadership who look like or relate to the customers and clients you serve?
- ➢ Do the vision, mission, and goals reflect equitable inclusion of diverse people?
- ➢ Are performance and risk management systems sensitized to implicit bias?
- ➢ Are policies and procedures sensitized to implicit bias?
- ➢ What kind of DEI metrics are captured relating to each level of the Organizational Performance System?
- ➢ Are metrics reported regularly to the Board?
- ➢ Does the Board challenge leadership when metrics are not meeting expectations?

Transformational Change

Transformational change is about moving the entire organization to a different way of behaving and being. Questions to ask include:

- ➢ Is there and a sense of urgency to implementing DEI?
- ➢ Are key stakeholders visibly pushing for DEI?
- ➢ Is there a vision for DEI?
- ➢ Is information about DEI constantly communicated from the top of the organization?
- ➢ Do leaders remove obstacles to the new vision?
- ➢ Are there systematic plans for creating short-term wins?
- ➢ What ongoing programs, products, or services can incorporate DEI?

To answer these questions, we need to gather data. We look at sources of data, gathering data, and drawing conclusions from the data (i.e., turning it into actionable information). Head of HR Colleen Clark of Life is Good describes that they have a 2-part measurement of organizational performance:

1. Pulse survey (3 questions out of 20 are around equity – just added) and use Culture Amp to look at industry positions.
2. Company performance to our Earnings Before Interest, Taxes, Depreciation, and Amortization (EBIDA).

Sources of data I have found most effective in understanding the current status include the following:

➤ **HR Information Systems** for demographic information. Ballentine Partners recently moved to a new payroll system - Chronos Workforce Ready Platform and are now tracking things like offers to diverse candidates.

➤ **Staff/Employee/Board Surveys (annual and/or "pulse")** for information on whether people feel like they are included and/or belong which reflects how relevant the organization is. Denise Lamoreaux of Atos shared: "We do an annual employee survey. And there are specific diversity centered questions asked about role models about engagement in our diversity programs, and things along those lines. And we have seen steady increases in the percentage of people who respond favorably and really feel our diversity programs are contributing to their employee well-being."

➤ **Customer/Client Surveys** for information on how well the products or services meet the needs of diverse people, which reflects how effective and relevant the organization is.

> **Management Survey** for information about how well diverse people are being included toward igniting organizational performance, which reflects how efficient the organization is.

> **Interviews with Board, Staff, Customers and Clients, Suppliers, Community Leaders and Members** for more in-depth information and insights into what's going on (i.e., more than what we would gather just through a survey). This reflects how efficient, effective, and relevant the organization is.

> **Focus Groups**, again, for more in-depth information and insights and to allow for "riffing" of new ideas improvised from general conversation.

Obviously, there are pros and cons to each data source. My experience is that the same guidelines for gathering data about any topic apply for gathering data about DEI. The differences I have seen in gathering data around DEI have to do with the following.

> In many cases, the data does not exist. For example, many organizations do not capture demographic data about their staff.

> There are laws about what and/or how you can ask around demographics.

Remember that Chapter 12 identified questions that can be a guide for identifying the impact of DEI on the organization. Exhibit 13.5 describes those questions and the data sources from which answers can be identified.

Exhibit 13.5. Data Source(s) for DEI Impact

Question	Data Source(s)
How does DEI contribute to delivery of organization performance goals (effectiveness/relevance)?	> Customer/Client Surveys > Interviews with Board, Staff, Customers/Clients, Suppliers, Community > Focus Groups
How are DEI considerations incorporated into decisions on key	> Staff/Employee Surveys

topics such as members, services, and location (efficiency)?	
How are leaders held accountable for DEI results (Effectiveness)?	➢ Staff/Employee Surveys ➢ Management Survey
What mechanisms are in place to monitor and respond to what is working - and what is not? (Efficiency/Financial Viability)	➢ Staff/Employee Surveys ➢ Customer/Client Surveys ➢ Interviews with Board, Staff, Customers/Clients, Suppliers, Community ➢ Focus Groups
How effectively do programs create a more inclusive environment, and not only a more diverse one? (effectiveness)	➢ Staff/Employee Surveys ➢ Interviews with Board, Staff, Customers/Clients, Suppliers, Community

The process of data gathering involves the following.

➢ Understanding the organization's business goals and objectives or mission in the nonprofit sense.

➢ Creating the questions that tie back to the organization's goals.

➢ Finalizing the data gathering strategy which includes:

• Interview strategy: identifying the different stakeholders to be interviewed;

• Survey strategy which involves the following decisions.

o Do you need to create separate surveys for board versus staff? I have done it both ways: a survey for the Board and staff and a survey for the Board that is separate from staff. Which way works best depends upon the type of Board you have. A purely "advisory" Board should have a separate survey. An "active" Board (where the Board members are not only advising leadership but actually doing the work of the organization - usually for smaller nonprofits) can be part of the Staff survey.

- o How are we surveying the people being served? All online? Some on paper? The answer here depends on the level of access to the Internet people have. For example, people served at a food pantry most likely do not have access to a computer they would need to have hardcopy surveys.
- o Do volunteers receive a set of questions different from those asked of the staff?
- o Do we survey managers separately from individual contributors? For flat organizations where there are not too many levels, managers and individual contributors can be surveyed together.
- o What geographical considerations are there? If the organization is large enough that there are multiple campuses and multiple cities, then we want to survey people in multiple locations.
- o What percentage of diverse personalities do we want to interview in terms of race, ethnicity, age, gender, political persuasion, thinking styles?
- o Should we hold focus groups? And if so, who should be part of the Focus Groups? Focus groups allow you to gain insights into cross-functional interactions with respect to equity and inclusion. They are valuable if you have a larger organization or many levels within your organization.

➤ Managing Challenges & Risk involves identifying what challenges you might face in gathering data and creating strategies to overcome them. Exhibit 13.7 can help with this.

➤ Communicating the effort: The fact that you are doing this analysis and gathering this data needs to be communicated. Communication is what gives people the understanding that DEI is a priority. When they hear about it frequently from leadership, they understand it is a priority.

➤ Gathering data: scheduling interviews, holding interviews, sending out those surveys, holding focus groups, doing data analysis, and reporting out those findings.

Exhibit 13.6. Data Gathering Challenges & Approaches

Challenge	Issue/Approach
Scheduling interviews	Scheduling interviews can take time. To simplify and streamline interview scheduling, I have used calendly.com. I created a special scheduler for scheduling interviews that was linked to my calendar. The link to this scheduler was sent to potential interviewees. The interviewees selected an interview time and that time was automatically reserved on my calendar.
Small number of people from which to gather data	Consider that not everyone invited to provide input will agree to share their opinions. So, that will reduce the number of completed surveys or interviews. So, you may wish to "oversample" to get a useful number of responses.
Badly coded HRIS system data	Recognize that some data is not available or codded in an HRIS System. For example, during one data gathering exercise we discovered that the Sr. Vice-President of the organization, who was African-American, was not properly coded in the HRIS. We took this into consideration as we analyzed the data.
Over/underrepresentation in job categories	As there is less diversity in higher ranks of most organizations, we must be careful not gather data from diverse people in as many job levels as possible.
Consistent Interview Protocol	Multiple interviewers may perform interviews differently. This can influence the interviewee's responses and mar the results. Create a script that is used by every interviewer.
Coding of result data	This is a challenge regardless of the topic of surveys. If your survey gathers data in open

	questions vs. multiple choice, how will you aggregate /summarize responses.
Previous survey style/bias/ contradiction	Those involved may be accustomed to a certain style survey from the organization. Use that same style if possible. Also, be wary that respondents may suffer from "survey fatigue" if they have already responded to a survey in roughly the past week.
Socially acceptable answers.	Some people may give socially responsible responses rather than sharing what they really feel. Ask for honest responses in the beginning of the survey/interview and explain that the responses are kept confidential.
Incentives	One philosophy to increase responses to surveys or interviews is to give some kind of reward or incentive. Whether you give a reward or incentive depends upon whether you have done so in the past or if you want to set a precedent for future surveys or interviews.

There may be others challenges specific to your organization. Create your own chart and include them.

Drawing Conclusions

Analyzing data to draw conclusions is accomplished using an approach used by data analytics expert Julie Alig, Ph.D.

➤ "Look for patterns, patterns, patterns, patterns. Look for trend patterns over time." Look for patterns in retention of different groups of employees. She says "Patterns are your friend." For example, are there more ideas flowing from diverse staff than there were last year? That indicates diversity is, in fact, being included.

➤ Look for information that not only proves what you were expecting to see, but also look for things that disprove what you are expecting to see. This critical analysis fosters trust with your audience. You're not trying to drive an agenda, necessarily. Looking for things that disprove what you are expecting to see also acts as a failsafe against your own biases. As we said earlier, we are human animals, and our brains are wired a certain way such that there are biases in how we perceive and understand things. This can cause interpretations of the data which are not totally accurate or true.

➢ Think critically about what questions your data can and cannot answer. At the end of the day, you might want to be able to say something about an area but the data doesn't exist or you are unable to collect it (for example, you send out a survey and only get a 1% response rate - and it's just not enough to draw any conclusions.)

➢ Benchmarking is very helpful. You might be in an industry where it's hard to benchmark yourself against other companies, so benchmark yourself against yourself, do it over time, do it by geographic location. If you're a company that has multiple locations, benchmark against yourself, again, as a way to set goals and see how you're progressing towards those goals.

➢ Disaggregate the data. Break down results into subgroups. For example, instead of looking only at the aggregate of your employees, break the data down by sexual orientation, or gender orientation (male, female, non-binary), by race, thinking style.

Conclusions should be documented in a report. The report analyzes the data gathered through the previously describes processes and covers the following:

➢ The answers to the high-level questions described in Chapter 12.
➢ A SWOT analysis with respect to DEI.
➢ A description of the organization's status with respect to each of the goals based on what was discussed in Chapter 12. For example, a chart similar to that shown in Exhibit 13.7 could be used to show data related to representation goals. The blue bar could represent

your industry. You could add a yellow in this bar to show where your organization is today. Thus, in one image, you are presenting your organization rates as they relate to your industry rates and the rates in other industries. This can tell you if you are ahead of or behind others in your industry – which might tell you if you need to take steps to improve your status in this area.

➤ Recommendations on what should be done to move up the DEI maturity levels. For example, training on DEI so that all employees see DEI as a core competency moving up from Emerging to Basic.

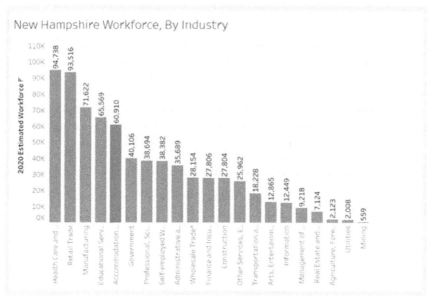

Exhibit 13.7. Workforce Industry Comparison

➤ Recommendations on how to progress toward DEI goals should be tracked. Whatever goals you identify, consider using a balanced scorecard method to tracking DEI efforts. Armando Llorente explains that one successful effort in which he was involved chose to "visualize our scorecard on a quarterly basis, because we had the MBO that said, okay, what's happened from a product, profitability, business development, staffing."

There are many measurement systems used by organizations. They are divided into two general categories: leading indicators and lagging indicators. An example of the balanced scorecard framework shown in Exhibit 13.8 is one of these measurement systems used by many. It can be used to track progress toward achieving the stated DEI goals from the perspectives of Financial/Stakeholders, Customer, Internal Business Processes, and Learning & Growth.

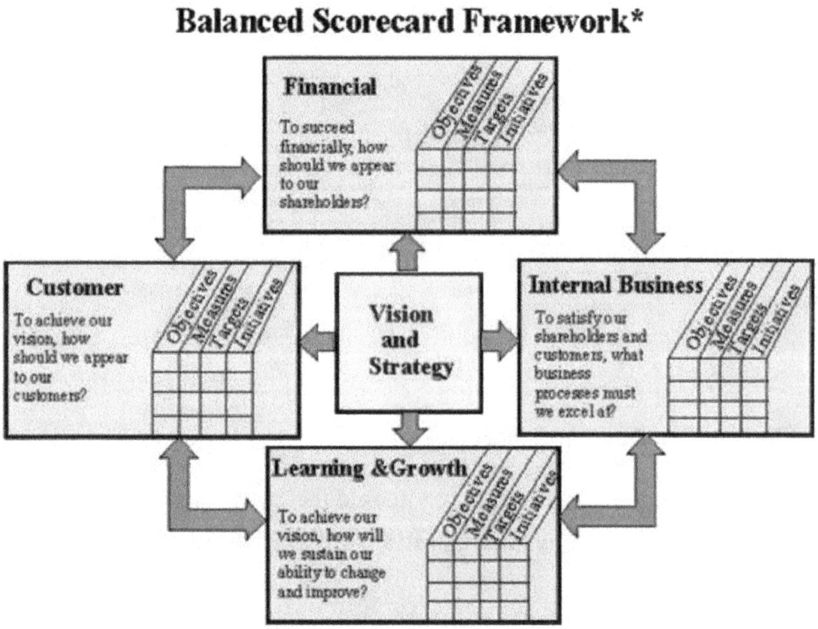
Balanced Scorecard Framework*
Financial
To succeed financially, how should we appear to our shareholders?
Objectives
Measures
Targets
Initiatives
Customer
To achieve our vision, how should we appear to our customers?
Vision and Strategy
Internal Business
To satisfy our shareholders and customers, what business processes must we excel at?
Learning &Growth
To achieve our vision, how will we sustain our ability to change and improve?

Exhibit 13.8. Balanced Scorecard Example

For example, the Customer card could show data on satisfaction of diverse customers. The Internal Business Processes card could show the percentage of business processes that have been updated to have an equity lens. The Learning & Growth card could show data on the number of people trained in DEI. Balanced Scorecards that focus specifically on DEI are sometimes referred to as "Diversity Scorecards."[117]

The Balanced Scorecard Framework is a static view of the organization. Consider also using a method that shows progress over time, as shown in Exhibit 13.9.

Companies do a better job of increasing diversity when they forgo the control tactics and frame their efforts more positively. The most effective programs spark engagement, increase contact among different groups, or draw on people's strong desire to look good to others.

% CHANGE OVER FIVE YEARS IN REPRESENTATION AMONG MANAGERS

Type of program	White		Black		Hispanic		Asian	
	Men	Women	Men	Women	Men	Women	Men	Women
Voluntary training			+13.3		+9.1		+9.3	+12.6
Self-managed teams	-2.8	+5.6	+3.4	+3.9				+3.6
Cross-training	-1.4	+3.0	+2.7	+3.0	-3.9		+6.5	+4.1
College recruitment: women*	-2.0	+10.2	+7.9	+8.7		+10.0	+18.3	+8.6
College recruitment: minorities**			+7.7	+8.9				
Mentoring				+18.0	+9.1	+23.7	+18.0	+24.0
Diversity task forces	-3.3	+11.6	+8.7	+22.7	+12.0	+16.2	+30.2	+24.2
Diversity managers		+7.5	+17.0	+11.1		+18.2	+10.9	+13.6

*College recruitment targeting women turns recruiting managers into diversity champions, so it also helps boost the numbers for black and Asian-American men.

**College recruitment targeting minorities often focuses on historically black schools, which lifts the numbers of African-American men and women.

NOTE GRAY INDICATES NO STATISTICAL CERTAINTY OF A PROGRAM'S EFFECT.
SOURCE AUTHORS' STUDY OF 829 MIDSIZE AND LARGE U.S. FIRMS. THE ANALYSIS ISOLATED THE EFFECTS OF DIVERSITY PROGRAMS FROM EVERYTHING ELSE GOING ON IN THE COMPANIES AND IN THE ECONOMY.
FROM "WHY DIVERSITY PROGRAMS FAIL," BY FRANK DOBBIN AND ALEXANDRA KALEV, JULY-AUGUST 2016   © HBR.ORG

Exhibit 13.9. Example Diversity Trend Graphic

Organization Communications

Communications are key to making people feel as if they are in the know and that the issue is important. Questions to ask include:

➢ Are there regular, frequent communications about DEI from the leadership?

➢ Are multiple communications channels used to talk about DEI?

➢ Are communications about DEI sent outside the organization?

Key reader takeaways

The Do phase begins with creating a project plan structure that will ensure tasks will be identified and completed. Identifying the gaps between the current state and the DEI vision, mission, and goals identified in Chapter 12 is accomplished by identifying a high-level series of questions and asking for information about all of the organizational performance system levels. Surveys, HRIS, interviews, and focus groups are the ways data is gathered to answer the questions identified.

An analysis is then performed on the information gathered. The results of the analysis are presented in a report that provides conclusions about where the organization is today and recommends changes to the organization to move it toward DEI.

Consider This...

This chapter explored the current state of the organization and what steps it might take to improve how it equitably include diverse people.

- ➢ What is your organization's readiness to implement a DEI program?
- ➢ Is everyone in your organization trained on how to include diverse perspectives in decision making?
- ➢ Does your organization have a decision-making process that ensures inclusion of different perspectives?

Do decisions about how the buildings that the organization either operates or exists in consider societal impact? Environmental impact?

The thesis of this chapter was that performing a current state analysis is critical to knowing what needs to be changed. This chapter covered the beginning of the Do phase of the Organizational Performance Through Diversity Roadmap which describes how to perform a current state analysis. Here are some questions you should ask yourself to see if you are ready to move on:

Question	Your Response
Do you understand what goes into assessing an organization's current state of DEI?	

Do you understand the way the DEI Program Schedule evolves over time?	
Do you understand the difference between short-term change and transformational change?	
Do you understand how to track progress toward DEI?	

If you answered "yes" to these questions, then you're ready to move on to the next chapter, which discusses designing and making changes to the organization toward DEI and superior organizational performance.

CHAPTER 14

Do - Make Change

"Vision without action is merely a dream. Action without vision just passes the time. Vision with action can change the world."

—Joel A. Barker

Thesis: *Organizational Change must be intentionally designed to be effective and long-lasting.*

Design Change Toward DEI

The previous chapter described how to assess the gaps between your vision of DEI in the organization and where the organization is today. The answers to those questions should be used to design and implement changes to center DEI throughout the organization.

Actions should take place within the organization, within the community, and within society. High-level examples of actions in those areas are shown in Exhibit 14.1,[118]

Exhibit 14.1. Example Actions to Center DEI

Within the Organization	Within the Community	Within Society
➢ Embedding accountability throughout the organization ➢ Designing HR policies and practices that are actively inclusive and equitable, not merely not discriminatory ➢ Expanding power and voice to designing products and services that center equitable outcomes	➢ Authentically build trust and relationships ➢ Redesign corporate philanthropy to address structural problems ➢ Advocate for local policies that address structural inequities ➢ Support environmental justice	➢ Take on national-level public policy, lobbying, and advocacy to advance racial equity ➢ Make investments to promote equity ➢ Transform communications to advance racial equity

The identification of the actual actions is discussed in this chapter. Those actions identified will be included in the Program Schedule previously initiated as described in Create Initial Program Schedule.

Stakeholder Value Delivery

To improve Stakeholder Value Delivery, consider designing the following actions:

➢ Performing industry trend analysis with an equity lens.
➢ Discovering what diverse customers and other stakeholders value.
➢ Translating that value proposition into products and services that create an experience the customers and other stakeholders value.

Technical Core Competencies and Financials

Policies and procedures ensure consistent execution of processes. In addition to using an equity lens on processes themselves, an equity lens should be applied to all policies and procedures of the organization. In addition, there should be at least one separate policy and procedure on how to report discrimination and what will be done to address that report in a fair, transparent manner that prevents retaliation.

To improve Technical Core Competencies and Financials, consider designing the following:

> ➤ The technical requirements for your business or industry segment so that your products or services are not solely White Normative;
> ➤ The key performance requirements for products and services so they resonate with for diverse audiences;
> ➤ Update of at least the ten top core business processes (if not all of your processes) to have an equity lens;
> ➤ Identification of the technical capabilities and key positions required in a way that is sensitive to diverse people.

Organizational Performance Drivers

This section describes the possible actions in each of the Organizational Performance Drivers.

Strategic & Business Model

To improve the Strategic & Business Model, consider designing the following:

> ➤ Creation of Strategic Goals with people who have diverse perspectives;
> ➤ Performing competitive analysis with a wide variety of perspectives;
> ➤ Identifying the Business Model from a wide variety of perspectives;
> ➤ Identifying vision and mission with people from a wide variety of perspectives;
> ➤ Identifying values and principles with people from a wide variety of perspectives.

Leadership

To improve Leadership, leaders need to be developed. Leaders also need to understand decision making.

Leadership Development

To improve leadership, consider putting all leaders through inclusive leadership development.

All leaders go through an inclusive leader development continuum.[119] The continuum consists of development phases that show a progression in understanding how to be inclusive. The phases (aka stages) are:

Phase 1: Unaware—Initially, you are unaware of diversity and its value. You think diversity is compliance related—i.e., something the government makes you do. You think it is simply about tolerating others—to the middle of our Diversity Behavior Continuum. Ensuring that diversity, equity, and inclusion happens is someone else's job, not yours, so it is not worth paying attention to.

Phase 2: Aware—You are aware that you have a role to play in DEI and are educating yourself as to how best to move forward at the interpersonal level. The levers available to you at this stage of your development are:

- ➤ Show respect for the opinion of every employee
- ➤ Keep quiet when appropriate
- ➤ Challenge assumptions
- ➤ Have empathy, arts, and humor
- ➤ Interrupt bias

Phase 3: Active—You have shifted your priorities and are finding your voice as you begin to take meaningful action that supports others. This is moving away from the autocratic management style mentioned in Chapter 8: What Are the Challenges to Igniting Organizational Performance Through Diversity. You have shifted from acting in a private way to acting in a public way. The levers available to you at this stage are:

- ➤ Mentor and sponsor

➤ Show vulnerability
➤ Tap into your "why"
➤ Being cognizant of the unique challenges faced by a diverse person and being available to help them through these challenges[120]

Angela Peacock posits that "You can only claim to have the solid foundations of an inclusive environment if your leaders are:

➤ Attending employee resource group (ERG) meetings;
➤ Working with recruiters who can deliver candidates from a more diverse set of backgrounds;
➤ Clear on the reasons they are putting one employee and not another forward for a project;
➤ Demonstrating and developing their non-performative allyship."[121]

Phase 4: Advocate—You are proactively and consistently confronting discrimination. You are using that equity lens and ensuring that everyone is using that equity lens. You are working to bring about change in order to prevent discrimination on a systemic level by changing policies and procedures through evaluating how policies and procedures are being implemented and followed.

The levers available to you at this stage are:

➤ Interrogate norms with the goal of leveling the playing field at work and in life in a general
➤ Identify and work to correct systemic inequities

These stages somewhat model the PwC DEI Organizational Maturity model levels. Unaware and Emerging are the lowest levels where the organization and people in the organization are unaware of what DEI is or its value. Advocate and Differentiating are the highest levels where the organization and people in the organization are strategic and proactive when it comes to DEI. They exhibit equitable inclusion of diverse people as a core competency and leverage it to improve organizational performance.

Decision-Making Guidelines

To improve decision-making, consider designing the following:

- ➤ A decision-making model as described in the above section on Leadership.
- ➤ A review of the Clark Equity Decision Making tool.[122]
- ➤ Purchase of Critical Thinking Cards or products from sources such as the Thinking Shop.[123]
- ➤ A decision-making process with a built-in equity lens for the entire organization.

Organization & Operating Model

To improve the organization and Operating Model, consider designing:

- ➤ jobs in a structure that does not rely on personality characteristics.
- ➤ targets for what diversity dimensions should be part of the executive team. For example, Atos took a number of actions in this regard which helped them increase the number of women as executives from 13% at the beginning of the 2020 to 30% by the end of 2020:
  - added roles in Project Management and Quality Management to their "Executive Team";
  - Created specific communities within the company. One is called the Experts Community;
  - Created development opportunities through programs with Google and Microsoft

Human Capital

To improve Human Capital, keep these strategy precepts in mind:

1. Know your community
2. Prepare for Diversity (Policies & Procedures)
3. Recruit with intention
4. Hire with intention

5. Retain with sensitivity

Consider designing actions in each of the Howes' areas of Human Capital:

➢ Selection (attract, recruit, interview)
➢ Hire
➢ Retain

Selection - Attract

To attract diverse candidates, consider designing the following actions:[124]

➢ **Internal to the organization**: Ensure that policies and procedures create a welcoming culture free from implicit bias.

➢ **External to the organization – reputation**: create a reputation that the organization is welcoming, inclusive, and a place to grow. Examples:

- Hold sessions (as Atos did) where people present what made them get into science and showcased women.

- Sponsor or fund programs and organizations that serve people from disadvantaged backgrounds.

- Partner with non-profits that create opportunities and advance the rights of underrepresented populations.

- Create a mentorship program.

- Reexamine your employee referral program.

- Create a diversity and inclusion policy.

- Make diversity and inclusion a core part of your company's culture.
- Remove unintentionally biased language from job descriptions.
- Highlight your company's commitment to diversity.
- Translate brochures & informational material.
- Ensure senior leadership is committed to diversity.

➢ **External to the organization - community:**

- Gain an understanding of the community(s) in which your organization operates.
- Gain an understand the demographics of your community.
- Make sure the community is ready to support diverse people and provide the products and services that will allow them to lead the lives they want to live. There are examples of people of color who took a job in New Hampshire, only to leave because they couldn't find the products and services that they wanted, such as a barber. Their leaving had nothing to do with the job itself but everything to do with the community in which they had to live that could not provide what they needed.

Selection – Recruit

 At Atos, part of the recruiting strategy is to be able to say they have won awards around the key target diversity areas. They spent less than $1000 in 2021 for awards applications and have been recognized by several organizations as a leading organization in DEI, including in the top 100 on the Stonewall Workplace Equality Index.

To recruit diverse candidates, consider designing the following actions:[125]

➢ Make sure the job descriptions:

- Show what non-work benefits/clubs are available, specifically for PoC.

- Focuses on the top competencies needed for the vacant position based on the job description.
- Uses bias-free (e.g. gender-neutral[126]) language
- Includes training and development. In addition to the traditional enticements, training and development can also be a recruitment tool. "To attract and retain talent, the companies around the world sare taking a multipronged approach. In addition to wage increases, more than one-third in North America; Asia Pacific; and Europe, the Middle East, and Africa are offering training, mentoring, and skills development."[127]

➤ Think outside of the box to reach diverse candidates. "Old-school sourcing channels produced stellar results for Edward Thompson at previous employers. Those channels included reaching out to local churches and running ads for bilingual roles in ethnic community newspapers. Experimenting with a mix of old and new—including virtual hiring events—was also "hugely successful."[128]

➤ Consider that we are in one of the tightest labor markets in memory, and all industries are feeling the pressure. Companies are getting increasingly desperate, but desperation can spark new ways of thinking about how to fill vacancies. An often-overlooked group is retirees, who represent a largely untapped source of promising talent to help stem the impacts of the Great Resignation. Think about hiring retirees.[129]

➤ Recruiting resources should include some or all of the following which are highlighted by consultant Lila Kelly in her Diversity Recruiting Resource and Directory:
  - Community agencies and organizations
  - Community events of diverse groups
  - Professional associations of diverse groups
  - Colleges and universities of predominantly diverse groups
  - Education field – urban teach programs

- Job fairs in areas where there are diverse groups
- Newspaper/magazines/journals of diverse groups
- Radio stations and programs of diverse groups
- Web sites, webcasts, podcasts and other online channels of diverse groups

➤ Good recruiters know how to target passive job seekers because of the lack of qualified job candidates to fill critical roles. Locating, wooing, and successfully luring passive job seekers is critical for organizations to remain competitive in a tight labor market. [130]

Selection - Interviewing

To interview diverse candidates, best practice is to prepare for the interviews before conducting the interviews.

Nannan Hu shared, "We ensured that our recruiters and hiring managers engaged with people based on their background. We made sure that once minorities were in the interview process, they don't fall out because of unconscious implicit bias. Our software instituted a blind interview processes depersonalizing candidate resumes (name, address, etc.)."

To improve interviews, consider designing the following to limit the impact of implicit bias:[131]

➤ Mask faces and names in applications and resumes before review
➤ Hold initial interviews over the phone to create blind first impressions.
➤ Take steps to de-bias yourself and anyone in the interview process.
➤ Choose the best type of assessments/work sample tests
➤ Consider "likability" - just because someoneis likeable does not mean they can do the job well
➤ Practice interviewing

To improve the conducting of interviews, consider designing the following actions:[132]

1. Inform the interviewer about the DEI goals of the organization.
2. Require more than one interviewer to be present in the interview room to create the opportunity for multiple assessments/interpretations of candidates.
3. Ensure that each candidate is interviewed by more than one person.
4. Allow applicants to discuss and/or demonstrate what they can offer the organization.
5. Always check with the candidate if there is a need for any specific arrangements (e.g., physical access, interpreters, etc.) for the interview.
6. Have questions prepared in advance, but rely on a relational style to get deeper into important discussions.
7. Ensure consistency and fairness in questioning focusing on the real needs of the job.
8. Allow the interviewee time to make their point.
9. Do not ask invasive and irrelevant questions (e.g., 'Do you intend to have a family?') even if it is legal.
10. Keep records of questions and answers.
11. Do not use stereotyped or discriminatory language or discriminatory requirements (e.g., 'salesman,' 'age 30-45 years').
12. If used, ensure recruitment consultants are fully briefed on your requirements and have a good understanding of equal opportunity and anti-discrimination principles.
13. Ensure that a diverse group of employees are part of the hiring decision.

Hire

Hiring includes the acts of agreeing to an employer/employee (volunteer) relationship, and Onboarding/New Hire indoctrination.

Agreements

The agreement process should ensure that the candidate understands the cultural norms for agreements and employer/employee relationships in the country and region in which you operate. This will minimize issues with expectations as some cultures have different norms for agreements and employment.

Onboarding

It is important to have a new hire/onboarding process for employees and volunteers. The components of a good onboarding process[133] are shown in Exhibit 14.3. These steps should be tailored to the diverse people just as job descriptions are tailored.

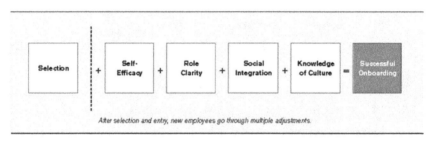

Exhibit 14.3. New Hire/Onboarding Process

To help diverse people feel like they belong and are welcome, the new hire/onboarding process should include the following:[134]

> Discussion on organization culture and norms (i.e., expectations for how to represent the department with the public, communication norms, any expectations on appearance and time).

> Overview of racial equity work, organization functions, and how decisions are made in your organization.

> Connection with a "buddy" or informal mentor to help learn more about what to expect when working for the department.

➤ Connection to activities and networks like affinity groups, lunch and learn sessions, employee gatherings based on their interests.

Retain

Retention is impacted by maintaining an inclusive culture, career development, growth opportunities (promotion), and reward.

Inclusive Culture

Armando Llorente shared the story of an organization he worked with on creating an inclusive culture. This organization wanted to make sure managers were "tuned in" to what was going on with respect to DEI. They had extensive training sessions for managers specifically, so that they were able to better understand and embrace the philosophy of DEI and the responsibilities that were on their shoulders for purposes of building an inclusive workplace and really understanding differences.

After the training, the way the managers spoke with diverse employees changed. The managers talked with members of the African-American groups, the Asian-American groups and the Hispanic groups and relayed that they each had great knowledge and great ideas but were relatively quiet during meetings. The managers actually asked what they could do to get people to be "a little bit more vocal and then take a more active role"? One of the Asian-American colleagues said that that no one had really ever asked for such input when they were in team meetings. An Asian-American said that the manager asked, "Anyone have any questions?" And since she really didn't have any questions, she was quiet. But she said, had you asked me about "my thoughts on a particular initiative, I would have gladly spoken up."

In the story above, the employee feels free to speak up when included (actively engaged).

Retention is increased when people feel they belong. Belonging can be enhanced by promoting allyship – amplifying the voice of those underrepresented so they feel they belong.[135] Ensure managers are aware of this.

To increase retention, consider designing ways to make people feel they belong. For example, Atos has pride month, a Disability Month, and other celebrations to recognize people and make them feel as if they belong, this makes them more productive and loyal. The company also has a millennials group.

Career Development

Atos has a program in place called Bridging the Generational Skills Gap—a joint venture between the D&I, Learning Development, and career management groups to:

> "...showcase the skill sets we need our employees to develop/enhance, the certifications we recommend that they possess, and the ways by which they can seek support in the career development process. It's geared towards employees 50+ since they're staying in the workplace 10-15 years longer than previous generations, but everyone is welcome to attend."

As Denise Lamoreaux, head of Diversity at Atos, shared:

> "I built it as a result of my participation in AARPs' Living, Learning, and Earning Longer program, and as a result of a report that stated that Germany, Italy, and Japan have the most employees over 55 in the world. We need to plan for retirement, but also for keeping our employees' skills relevant while they continue to work with us."

To improve career development, consider designing the following:[136]

- ➢ Up-to-date job descriptions for all roles at all levels; role, responsibilities, tasks, competencies, and essential Knowledge, Skills, and Abilities (KSAs) clearly stated.
- ➢ KPIs (key performance indicators) for individuals' contributions to team/group projects.
- ➢ Competency Models for all roles showing the paths to advancement for all positions; this information is easily available and accessible.
- ➢ Access to professional development training, mapped to the competency models for all positions in the organization.
- ➢ Career advancement supported through multiple pathways for skills and knowledge acquisition rather than through a single prescribed path.

Growth Opportunities (Promotion)

Armando Llorente shares that a successful tactic is to "create a nice diagram that says, you come into the company and here are the ways that you can grow. We had managers, and in this case, members of the C suite coming into the individual affinity group meetings is saying, 'here's what you can look forward to within our company, for purposes of you want to go down this path, or you want to go down this path, here's how we will support you.' And then that opened the doors for mentorships. And identifying mentors and or coaches for individuals in the company. That instead of having your manager be the one that was always telling you, this is what you need to do, etc."

To improve growth opportunities for diverse people, consider designing the following:[137]

- ➢ Managers are measured on encouraging their reports to seek promotions.
- ➢ Managers are required to provide written justification of their promotion decisions.

> Records are to be maintained on managers to track the demographics of who they promote.

> Records are to be maintained on managers to track the demographics of who they do not promote.

> Specific goals are to be established regarding the number or percentage of diversity promotions.

> Specific goals are to be made public regarding the number or percentage of diversity promotions achieved.

Reward

To improve the Reward system, consider designing the following:

> Pay equity for diverse people in terms of compensation, bonuses, and promotions are tied, in part, to how well an organization retain employees from underrepresented demographics.

> Respectful communications which are critical to retain Generations Y and Z. "According to survey responses of more than 1,000 workers age 21 to 34, respectful interactions with managers are what they value most."[138]

High-Performing Culture

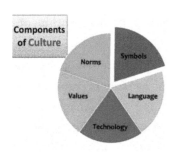

To get the best innovation and decision making, leaders need to make their interactions inclusive. Create a "safe space" for everyone to comment. Armando Llorente says that leaders in meetings can say, "here's what we're trying to do. I'm really interested in your feedback and your perspectives. This is a safe zone, meaning that no idea is going to be bad."

Having said this, one should not expect that diverse people will immediately feel comfortable speaking up on their own after just one such interaction. Armando indicates that it can take several months before diverse people achieve that level of comfort and trust.

To cultivate a High-Performing Culture, consider designing the following.

> ➢ Policies and procedures that create a welcoming culture free from implicit bias;
> ➢ A decision-making model that uses a process that is inclusive and equitable[139];
> ➢ An organization structure that makes role or responsibilities clear;
> ➢ Management techniques are used that ensure clarity of work;
> ➢ A Performance Management system that measures progress and ensures accountability for equitable inclusion of diverse people;
> ➢ A wellness plan customized for diverse people that minimizes burnout; team-building tools that encourage a winning attitude among diverse employees.

Governance & Management Systems

To improve Governance & Management Systems, consider designing the following:

> ➢ Ensure your organization's Board is diverse and representative of the stakeholders and customers/clients.
> ➢ Validate that mission/vision/goals reflect equitable inclusion of diverse people.
> ➢ Ensure the Board reviews DEI effort progress regularly and challenge leadership when metrics are not being met.
> ➢ Assemble a DEI Advisory Group with diverse representation.
> ➢ Establish an equity-based performance management system where an individual's goals align with the organization's DEI goals. Those individual's goals should be included in the performance management system for accountability. For example, Fidelity has recognized that what inclusion looks like differs for each person. So, they have incorporated into their performance management system that each employee should have their own Action Plan or goals with respect to DEI so that actions are aligned to enterprise goals.[140]

➢ Establish an organization-wide risk-management process that ensures inclusion of diverse people.

➢ Ensure the policies and compliance assessment process is completed by a diverse group of people.

➢ Identify a DEI leader/Champion to drive efforts across the organization. This will ensure that the effort does not fall off because it is not someone's official responsibility for which they are not being held accountable.

➢ Identify a senior management sponsor so that the effort is seen as an organizational high priority.

➢ Establish an Accountability Partner. This could be a consultant or an organization with established DEI expertise to help hold the organization accountable for its DEI work.

➢ Develop a statement of DEI values, principles, and/or commitments the organization will seek to uphold in achieving its mission. Note that just having a statement is not enough. As Aura Huot says, "You need to provide continuous feedback to employees about what is happening. The worse thing that can happen is no word about the effort after it has been announced. That is not good."

Organization Communications

To improve Organizational Communications. consider designing the following:

➢ A Communications Plan taking into consideration communication needs of diverse people (e.g., translated documents and events, audio clips for the blind).

➢ A Communications Plan with regular, frequent communications about DEI from the leadership.

➢ Multiple communications channels designed to reach diverse audiences inside and outside the organization.

Transformational Change

To improve Transformation Change toward DEI, consider designing the following:

> - Ways to support leaders removing obstacles to the new vision of DEI.
> - Systematic ways for creating and celebrating short-term wins.
> - Identifying when ongoing programs, products, or services can incorporate DEI.
> - Many organizations have traditionally trained on the topic of "diversity." But more organizations with which I have worked such as Fidelity, Velcro, HP are now starting to focus on "inclusion."
> - Delivery of DEI Training. As Aura Huot of Brensinger Architects makes the point that actual effort must be placed into the delivery of DEI training. Not just to "check the box" that training has been done, which people, who are all very smart, can see as just being performative. That mentality is the wrong mentality to have. You won't help the bottom line or the people in the organization. She says,"And overall, you're gonna end [up] losing the trust, and you're gonna lose in business, which is a problem."

Aura further goes on to talk about the importance of DEI training highlighting that training on DEI is, also, not a "one and done." It must be recurring just as compliance training is recurring. Otherwise, the learning loses its edge.

Some industries and professions have ethics guidelines and training that can help implement DEI. For example, in the healthcare industry, there is a focus on Biomedical ethics,[141] or the American Bar Association's Code of Ethics, or the Project Management Institute's Code of Ethics Professional Conduct. The list goes on and on.

Gail Manley from Fidelity shared that employees are at various points along the D&I journey. So, they put out a glossary of terms.

Schedule and Implement

To make the transformation actually happen, schedule the detailed DEI program actions identified and defined in this section above in the previously created Program Schedule and begin implementation of the designed program. To schedule and implement the design, consider the following:

➢ Develop project plans and milestones for each initiative.
➢ Create project teams, assigning team leads and members.
➢ Assign internal project sponsors and advisory teams.
➢ Integrate this Transformation Plan with the Business/Strategic Plan.
➢ Execute the actions for each initiative of the plan.
➢ Set up tracking mechanisms for all of the initiatives to transition into the Act/Adjust phase. (Note: setting up the tracking mechanisms can be done at the same time the schedule is developed.)
➢ Ensure those doing the work are trained in DEI and use of the Equity Lens **before** they begin their tasks.

Key reader takeaways

Designing and making changes requires discipline and the involvement of the entire organization. The operational performance system provides a useful framework for determining what has to be changed to increase organizational performance. The use of Project Management practices ensures the changes will be made efficiently and effectively.

Consider This...

This chapter explored executing a DEI program to ensure the entire organization equitably includes diverse people.

> ➤ Is everyone in your organization trained on how to include diverse perspectives in decision making?
> ➤ How well have your identified project management practices for your organization to schedule and implement cultural change?
> ➤ Has your organization linked cultural change to improvement in organizational performance?

The thesis of this chapter was that Organizational Change must be intentionally designed to be effective and long-lasting. This chapter described making actual changes to the organization that would be long-lasting. Here are some questions you should ask yourself to see if you are ready to move on:

Question	Your Response
Do you understand what goes into designing the changes to an organization to increase DEI?	
Do you understand the way the DEI Program Schedule evolves over time?	
Do you understand the difference between scheduling and implementing transformational change?	

If you answered "yes" to these questions, then you're ready to move on to the next chapter, which discusses checking the changes made to ensure they are having the desired impact and adjusting them to, as efficiently and effectively as possible, move the organization in the right direction toward DEI and superior organizational performance.

CHAPTER 15

Check and Act/Adjust

"What gets measured gets done"
—Tom Peters

Thesis: *Intentional steps need to be taken to ensure the changes to implement DEI are actually helping to achieve superior organizational performance.*

Airbnb is a wonderful example of testing a DEI effort to eliminate discrimination in sales.[142] It uses the technique of removing names from reservations, making them anonymous, just as we discussed removing names from resumes making them anonymous in Selection - Attract.

It is important to make sure the actions of the Program Schedule actually achieve the DEI goals established and do actually impact efficiency, effectiveness, relevance, and financial viability as intended. This chapter describes how to verify that the changes implemented had the desired impact and how to adjust the approach to DEI based on the changes that have not had the desired impact.

Check

How progress toward DEI and organizational performance should now be reviewed using whatever method you defined in the step as described in Chapter 13: Do - Current State Analysis. Again, the high-level questions to be answered are:

- ➢ How does DEI contribute to delivery of organization performance goals (effectiveness/relevance)?
- ➢ How are DEI considerations incorporated into decisions on key topics such as members, services, and location (efficiency)?
- ➢ How are leaders held accountable for DEI results (Effectiveness)?
- ➢ What mechanisms are in place to monitor and respond to what is working - and what is not? (Efficiency/Financial Viability)
- ➢ How effectively do programs create a more inclusive environment, and not only a more diverse one? (effectiveness)

A high-level report on these questions should be shared with the Board whenever they meet. This report could include a Balanced/Diversity Scorecard and a Diversity Trends Graphic. The Board should use these to "tweak" the general direction of the effort or to authorize more resources be applied in specific area.

More detailed reports should be shared in senior management meetings. These reports should be used by the teams to track progress and to "tweak" actions toward goals for which they are responsible or have major impact.

The above is checking progress of the DEI effort at a single point in time. It is also helpful to check progress toward moving up the PWC Maturity Curve (from Chapter 9, shown in Exhibit 9.1). This means asking questions such as:

- ➢ Do DEI programs, processes, and infrastructure foundations have some alignment with a talent lifecycle? And does a broader set of employees understand basic DEI concepts and their business value? (Emerging)

> ➤ Are programs, practices, and infrastructure more highly integrated with the talent lifecycle? And have some employees begun to internalize DEI and view it as a core competency? (Progressing)
>
> ➤ Do employees view DEI as essential to driving people and business performance? Is inclusion naturally embedded throughout all aspects of the employee and customer experience? (Differentiated)

Act/Adjust

When DEI program tasks are not having their desired impact or over time there is no movement up the PwC Maturity Curve, action should be taken to adjust the work being done. The change could be as simple as adding a Historically Black College or University (HBCU) to the list of locations that recruiters contact. Or it could be as complex as restructuring a part of the organization to eliminate a hostile workplace that is at risk for a sexual harassment suit.

These adjustments to project tasks should be captured using standard project management and management practices. A "Lessons Learned" process should be used to make recommendations for returning to the plan phase, so that there is continuous improvement in your organization.

Key reader takeaways

Checking the progress of tasks toward DEI requires discipline. Reports should be provided to the Board and senior management on a regular basis. The board and senior management should take these reports seriously and take action to adjust the work or the resources being applied when expectations are not being met.

Any adjustments to the plan should carry forth into the next Plan-Do-Check-Act/Adjust cycle starting at the beginning of the road map so there is a continuous improvement.

Consider This...

This chapter explored the validate implementation of plans to help the organization exhibit equitable inclusion of diverse people.

➤ Does your Board receive regular reports about large-scale initiatives that impact the entire organization?

➤ Does senior management receive regular reports on progress of projects and initiatives?

➤ Does your organization have processes for resources to be added or moved around when projects need more resources?

The thesis of this chapter was that intentional steps need to be taken to ensure the changes implementing DEI are actually helping to achieve superior organizational performance. This chapter described how to verify that planned changes are having their intended impact and how to adjust planned activities accordingly. Here are some questions you should ask yourself to see if you are ready to move on:

Question	Your Response
Do you understand how to check the impact of DEI efforts?	
Do you understand who should receive various type of progress reports?	
Do you understand what type of adjustments can and should be made to priest at list DEI plans?	

If you answered "yes" to these questions, then you're ready to move on to the next chapter, which ties everything together.

CHAPTER 16

Putting It All Together

"Diversity requires commitment. Achieving the superior
performance diversity can produce needs further action -
most notably, a commitment to develop a culture of
inclusion. People do not just need to be different; they need
to be fully involved and feel their voices are heard."
—Alain Dehaze

The thesis of this book is that diversity, equity, & inclusion is the way to gain a
competitive advantage and ignite superior organizational performance.

Stories and research highlight why diversity is important to address in an
organization. It is important from the perspectives of innovation,
sustainability, relevance, and financial viability. Organizations are made of
individuals. The way to have the impact the research indicates is possible,
is through recognizing that people are more likely to remain with an
organization and be more productive if the environment in which they
work make them feel as if they belong.

The term "diversity" is frequently defined as having Black people or women
in an organization. What we should really use as the definition of

"diversity" is the definition originally put forth by Marilyn Loden - people with diverse dimensions, attributes, or characteristics. Life-long dimensions such as race, age, or gender, etc. and malleable dimensions such as experiences, ways of interacting with the world such as income, geography, thinking styles, etc.

But beyond describing characteristics of an individual, the notion of diversity in organizations is really about equitable inclusion of diverse people so that they feel they belong bringing their authentic selves to work. Initiatives to create a welcoming/inclusive organization are referred to as Diversity, Equity, and Inclusion (DEI) initiatives. Sometimes "Belonging" is added to make the initiative name "DEIB". Sometimes Justice is added to make it Justice, Equity, Diversity, and Inclusion (JEDI). This is because having a diverse workforce itself is not sufficient to create welcoming/inclusive/high-performing organizations. And equitable treatment of individuals is really justice. My formula for organizational success that puts together these definitions is as follows - *"Welcoming/Inclusive/High-Performing organizations/societies exhibit equitable (not just equal) inclusion of diverse people."*

At a macro, societal, level, example signs of DEI include data showing at the industry level where regardless of their group: race, age, gender, disability, socioeconomic status, pay is equal. The ratio of the number of employees from various groups in various positions in organizations is on par with the number of people from those groups in society.

At the micro level, example signs of DEI in a particular organization include high employee satisfaction, ideas coming from diverse people, high average employee tenure. The PwC Maturity Curve provides a framework for discussing what DEI looks like for a particular organization.

Using a framework referred to as the Institutional and Organizational Assessment Model (IOA), Organizational Performance is described as being determined by effectiveness, efficiency, relevance, and financial viability. Achieving organizational performance is accomplished through the Organizational Performance System as defined Curt Howes. That system consists of the three (3) levels of: stakeholder value delivery, technical core competencies and financials, and Organizational Performance Drivers.

The challenges and barriers to achieving DEI can be viewed from both an interpersonal and organizational perspective. From the individual perspective, Implicit Bias is the root cause of not achieving DEI. It manifests as White Privilege/Normativeness in organizations and society through the way people interact with and behave around someone who is different than they are. From the organizational perspective, the barriers to achieving DEI have to do with culture and policies and procedures.

Given those challenges and barriers, creating a diverse workforce where everyone feels they belong and can perform at their best is no small feat. It takes a commitment to change. This kind of change can take months if not years to accomplish. It requires openness an intentionality on the part of everyone in the organization. And it requires a performance management system that holds everyone accountable for equitable inclusion of diverse people.

Achieving superior organizational performance through DEI requires an understanding of the levers that can be pulled on the journey to maturity on the PwC Maturity Curve. The curve shows increasing maturity in DEI starting at the Emerging level where DEI is, if at all addressed, addressed by a few individuals in the organization to the Differentiated level where DEI is embedded in everything the organization does.

DEI ignites superior organizational performance through improving the organizational performance system. Management style (moving from autocratic to permissive) is one of the most important levers that can be pulled on the journey to organizational performance through diversity. A Discovering Performance Through Diversity Roadmap based on the well-known Deming Plan-Do-Check-Act (PDCA) model can be used to move up the PwC Maturity Curve.

The Roadmap addresses DEI in each of the 3 levels of Howe's Organizational Performance System. The Roadmap can, and probably should be, repeated as long as the organization exists to make the organization more mature in its leveraging DEI thus moving up the PwC Maturity Curve. As the organization moves up the curve, performance should increase. The Roadmap high level milestones are:

- ➤ Planning the effort as a formal program
- ➤ Establishing an equitable and inclusive tone for the move toward DEI
- ➤ Analyzing the current state of the organization;
- ➤ Setting goals to guide where the organization should go;
- ➤ Defining understanding what could be done given the organization's resources will move the effort forward; her
- ➤ Executing a plan to make changes that will move the organization up the PwC Maturity Curve;
- ➤ Checking the progress of tasks toward DEI requires discipline and making adjustments to ensure the work actually has the intended impact.

Example Success Story

Following the advice and approaches in this book has led to improvements in organizational performance for several organizations. An example is a hospital with whom I recently worked.

The Board had made a statement making diversity a priority. The CEO and Senior VP had been through a diversity program offered by a local nonprofit so were versed in DEI issues. Working with the VP of Patient Health, we performed a Current State Analysis of the organization. We found that the organization had some diversity, but that diversity was not representative of the population it served. A non-discrimination policy existed, but the equity lens was not evident in operational policies and procedures. There was no Committee focused on DEI to guide the organization through improvements. They performed annual employee assessments and a survey of the community about the reputation of the institution. But leadership had not engaged with the community about DEIB.

Based on recommendations made at the end of the Current State Assessment, senior management chartered a DEIB Committee. The Committee establish DEI principles linked to the values of the organization which already related to equity and inclusion. These included:

> We will show respect for all people, embrace the diversity among us and engage in in open, honest, and difficult conversations to improve understanding and relationships.

> Inclusion and belonging are essential priorities for excellent patient care and we will collaborate as staff to demonstrate it.

> Education about diversity, equity, inclusion, and belonging will include awareness of trauma informed care, be available to all staff, and include participant engagement in its development and delivery.

> There will be a process for accountability and reconciliation when language or behavior that demonstrates bias occurs.

> Promoting equity will be a cornerstone in all areas of service delivery, patient experience, and community engagement.

They identified goals that supported the goals of the institution's strategic plan. The goals were:

> New education and training opportunities to increase awareness of DEIB at the leadership and staff levels will be developed.

> Identify employee and patient related policies from a DEIB perspective to identify gaps or necessary updates to align with the January 2019 Board resolution on Diversity and Inclusion.

> Participate in strategies with external partners to create communities in the region we serve more inclusive and welcoming for our staff and the population we serve.

Leadership engaged with the community helping to start an Equity Committee in the town. Community leaders such as the mayor, the head of the YWCA, and the Chamber of Commerce enthusiastically joined.

The results after one year were impressive. The annual Press Ganey survey showed a positive increase in results on several questions related to DEIB and efficiency. The organization is financially poised for long viability even as the population of the community, according to the 2020 Census, continues to become more diverse. The Community sees the institution as a leader in DEIB.

Consider This...

As you look to implement what you have learned from this book, I offer advice similar to that provided by Bari A. Williams in her book <u>Diversity in the Workplace: Eye-Opening Interviews to Jumpstart Conversations about Identify, Privilege, and Bias</u> along with some conversational norms I follow.

➢ Be considerate in how you discuss these topics with others in your organization. Approach those conversations with a spirit of curiosity, empathy, and seeking first to understand before seeking to be understood.

➢ Recognize these conversations as learning opportunities with something for everyone.

➢ Consider who is present and what potential emotional triggers might arise so you can create what Dr. Eric Law from the Kaleidoscope institute calls a "gracious space"[143] for the exchange of ideas where we can all be our authentic selves, learn, and grow.

➢ Remember that in implementing these ideas you will have difficult conversations about difficult topics. This requires everyone to acknowledge that discussions about diversity are likely to elicit strong emotions.

➢ Recognize and be sensitive to the vulnerability of minorities as well as the discomfort that people in positions of power might feel.

➢ Create spaces for everyone to process and feel the emotions that the conversations may spur. "Have your emotions or they will have you."[144]

> ➤ Use language that is appropriate to emphasize the idea that we need to become comfortable with discomfort.

> ➤ Help everyone recognize that not everyone has the appropriate language to articulate what they are feeling or observing. And that is OK as long as they are willing to learn.

> ➤ Check your biases at the door as they will invariably interfere with seeing a situation objectively.

> ➤ Don't take or give negative feedback as a personal attack. When everyone has what Dr. Carol Dwek from Stanford University calls a "Growth Mindset", everyone wins.

> ➤ Allow people to sit with their discomfort. People need time to digest what they have learned that is different from their beliefs and values or change will not "stick".

> ➤ Engage the resistance. Resistance is a sign that learning is taking place and change is "right around the corner".

> ➤ Meet people where they are. Not everyone has the same knowledge or experiences. We all learn and process information at different rates.

> ➤ Identify common beliefs. Starting from where people have things in common is proven to result in more productive conversations and work.

Call to Action

Now that you have seen how diversity can ignite superior organizational performance, here are some questions to ask yourself to see if you are ready for the journey.

Question	Your Response
Do you understand the definitions of the terms diversity, equity, inclusion, and organizational performance?	

Do you understand how to measure diversity, equity, inclusion toward organizational performance?	
Do you understand the signs and levers of DEI & Organizational Performance?	
Do you understand the steps along the Discovering Performance Through Diversity Roadmap to overcome the challenges and barriers to superior organizational performance?	

If you answered yes to these questions then you're ready to help drive a DEI effort in your organization that leads to superior organizational performance.

Endnotes

1. Edward E. Hubbard, <u>The Diversity Scorecard: Evaluating the Impact of Diversity on Organizational Performance</u>, (Jordan Hill: Elsevier, 2004), pg. 5.

2. Schumpeter, Joseph A., 1883–1950 (1983). Opie, Redvers, Elliott, John E., <u>The theory of economic development: an inquiry into profits, capital, credit, interest, and the business cycle</u>. New Brunswick, New Jersey, <u>ISBN</u> <u>0-87855-698-2</u>. OCLC <u>8493721</u>.

3. "Diversity, Equity and Inclusion 4.0: A toolkit for leaders to accelerate social progress in the future of work," World Economic Forum, June 23, 2020, <u>https://www.weforum.org/reports/diversity-equity-and-inclusion-4-0-a-toolkit-for-leaders-to-accelerate-social-progress-in-the-future-of-work</u>.

4. Vijay Eswaran ,"The business case for diversity in the workplace is now overwhelming," World Economic Forum , April 29, 2019, <u>https://www.weforum.org/agenda/2019/04/business-case-for-diversity-in-the-workplace</u>.

5. "Shaping the Sustainable Organization," Accenture , <u>https://www.accenture.com/us-en/insights/sustainability/sustainable-organization?c=acn_glb_buildingsustaingoogle_12379588&n=psgs_0921&gclid=Cj0KCQiAlMCOBhCZARIsANLid6a3BqVHnsvdjEefzDSgMm6F-DXUKlEIeKKDNniX8PbxUfnfQKf8y7AaAkZyEALw_wcB&gclsrc=aw.ds</u>.

6. "The business case for diversity in the workplace is now overwhelming," World Economic Forum article, April 29, 2019, <u>https://www.weforum.org/agenda/2019/04/business-case-for-diversity-in-the-workplace</u>.

7. "The Deloitte Global 2021 Millennial and Gen Z Survey," Deloitte, 2021 <u>https://www2.deloitte.com/global/en/pages/about-deloitte/articles/millennialsurvey.html</u>.

8. "The Age Diversity in the Workplace: How does it impact results?," *HR Magazine*, August 13, 2021, <u>https://www.hrcloud.com/blog/the-age-diversity-in-the-workplace-how-does-it-impact-results</u>.

9. William H. Frey, "What the 2020 census will reveal about America: Stagnating growth, an aging population, and youthful diversity," Brookings, April 26, 2021, <u>https://www.brookings.edu/research/what-the-2020-census-will-</u>

reveal-about-america-stagnating-growth-an-aging-population-and-youthful-diversity/.

10. Emily Schmall, "The Cult of Chick-fil-A," Emily Schmall, *Forbes,* July 6, 2007, https://www.forbes.com/forbes/2007/0723/080.html?sh=136b8d455971.

11. Andrea Coville, "3 Ways To Make Your Company Relevant," *Fast Company,* https://www.fastcompany.com/3028544/3-ways-to-make-your-company-relevant.

12. Thomas Baekdal, "Redefining Relevance: The Circles of Media," January 2019, https://www.baekdal.com/strategy/redefining-relevance-the-circles-of-media/.

13. Ibid.

14. Guy Powell, "MULTICULTURAL MARKETING CAMPAIGNS RAISE MARKETING ROI", https://prorelevant.com/multicultural-marketing/.

15. "Delivering Through Diversity," McKinsey & Company, https://www.mckinsey.com/business-functions/people-and-organizational-performance/our-insights/delivering-through-diversity, originally published in 2014 and updated in 2017.

16. Evan W. Carr, Andrew Reece, Gabriella Rosen Kellerman, and Alexi Robichaux, "The Value of Belonging at Work," *Harvard Business Review,"* December 16, 2019, http://hrb.org/2019/12/The-value-of-belonging.

17. Anna Brown, "5 key findings about LGBT Americans," Pew Research Center, June 13, 2017, https://www.pewresearch.org/fact-tank/2017/06/13/5-key-findings-about-lgbt-americans/.

18. "Gender identify and sexual orientation differences by generation," New Ipsos, February 23, 2021, https://www.ipsos.com/en-us/gender-identity-and-sexual-orientation-differences-generation.

19. "CDC: 53 million adults in the US live with a disability", July 30, 2015, https://www.cdc.gov/media/releases/2015/p0730-US-disability.html.

20. Josh Zumrum, "Not Just the 1%: The Upper Middle Class Is Larger and Richer than Ever," June 21, 2016, *The Wall Street Journal,* https://www.wsj.com/articles/BL-REB-35977.

21. "2021: The year in charts," December 17, 2021, https://www.mckinsey.com/featured-insights/2021-year-in-review/2021-the-year-in-charts?cid=other-eml-alt-mip-mck&hdpid=45e2232d-33d3-40eb-91ef-8a8803b7d3f6&hctky=12686677&hlkid=8d1bfd6cf1ed4ffb81107b4c0a43b972.

22. "Almost half of the Black US workforce is in lower-paying, frontline-service industries", McKinsey & Co., March 2, 2021, https://www.mckinsey.com/featured-insights/coronavirus-leading-through-the-crisis/charting-the-path-to-the-next-normal/almost-half-of-the-black-us-workforce-is-in-lower-paying-frontline-service-industries.

23. Dana M Peterson and Catherine L. Mann, "Closing the Racial Inequality Gaps," September 2020, CitiGPS, https://ir.citi.com/NvIUklHPilz14Hwd3oxqZBLMn1_XPqo5FrxsZDOx6hhil84Zxax EuJUWmak51UHvYk75VKeHCMI%3D.

24. Bryan Hancock, Monne Williams, James Manyika, Lareina Yee, and Jackie Wong, "Race in the Workplace: The Black Experience in the U.S. Private Sector," McKinsey & Co., https://www.mckinsey.com/featured-insights/diversity-and-inclusion/race-in-the-workplace-the-black-experience-in-the-us-private-sector?hdpid=8b6d0f4c-7bfb-41d1-bf26-500da2a9bf72&hctky=12686677&hlkid=2482380d5e24460dbc424c09c41a8c34.

25. Carol Fleck, "Forced Out, Older Workers Are Fighting Back," AARP, May 2014, https://www.aarp.org/work/on-the-job/info-2014/workplace-age-discrimination-infographic.html.

26. Juliana Menasce, Horowitz, Ruth Igielnik, and Rakesh Kochhar, "Most Americans Say There Is Too Much Economic Inequality in the U.S., But Fewer than Half Call It a Top Priority," Pew Research, January 9, 2020, https://www.pewresearch.org/social-trends/2020/01/09/most-americans-say-there-is-too-much-economic-inequality-in-the-u-s-but-fewer-than-half-call-it-a-top-priority/.

27. Kathy Caprino, "New Data Reveals the Hard Costs of Bias and How to Disrupt It," *Forbes,* October 2017, https://www.forbes.com/sites/kathycaprino/2017/10/26/new-data-reveals-the-hard-costs-of-bias-and-how-to-disrupt-it/?sh=7f20aa884595.

28. Jared Council, "2021 America's Best Employers For Diversity," April 26, 2022, https://www.forbes.com/best-employers-diversity/#4e679b7a9b9e.

29. "Pew Research Social & Demographic Trends: A Survey of LGBT Americans," Pew Research Center, June 13, 2013, http://www.pewsocialtrends.org/2013/06/13/a-survey-of-lgbt-americans/#fn-17196-1.

30. Kathy Caprino "New Data Reveals The Hard Costs Of Bias And How To Disrupt It," *Forbes,* October 26, 2017,

https://www.forbes.com/sites/kathycaprino/2017/10/26/new-data-reveals-the-hard-costs-of-bias-and-how-to-disrupt-it/?sh=32d142824595.

31. Erik van Vulpen, "A Practitioner's Guide to Organizational Effectiveness," the Academy to Innovative HR (AIHR) Digital, https://www.digitalhrtech.com/organizational-effectiveness/.

32. Vijay Eswaran, "The business case for diversity in the workplace is now overwhelming," World Economic Forum, April 29, 2019, https://www.weforum.org/agenda/2019/04/business-case-for-diversity-in-the-workplace/.

33. M. Christie Smith, PhD, Stephanie Turner, PhD, "The radical transformation of diversity and inclusion: The millennial influence," https://www2.deloitte.com/content/dam/Deloitte/us/Documents/about-deloitte/us-inclus-millennial-influence-120215.pdf.

34. "Physicians Assistant Book of Knowledge, 5th Edition.

35. Marilyn Loden and Judy Rosener, Workforce America!: Managing Employee Diversity as a Vital Resource, (Irwin 1990).

36. Lee Gardenswartz, Anita Rowe, "Four Layers of Diversity," https://www.gardenswartzrowe.com/why-g-r.

37. "The Nomad Economy," Korn Ferry, https://www.kornferry.com/content/dam/kornferry/docs/article-migration/Briefings38_Nomad-Economy.pdf.

38. Grant Suneson, "These states have the highest – and lowest – percentage of married people in the US," USA Today, March 7, 2019, https://www.usatoday.com/story/money/2019/03/07/marriage-us-states-highest-percentage-married-people/39043233/.

39. "New AMA policies recognize race as a social, not biological, construct", November 16, 2020, https://www.ama-assn.org/press-center/press-releases/new-ama-policies-recognize-race-social-not-biological-construct.

40. Resmaa Menachem, My Grandmother's Hands (Las Vegas: Central Recovery Press, 2017), pg. 245.

41. Felicity Menzies, "NINE CULTURAL VALUE DIFFERENCES YOU NEED TO KNOW," Include-Empower (blog), Culture Plus Consulting.com: https://cultureplusconsulting.com/2015/06/23/nine-cultural-value-differences-you-need-to-know/.

42. "Outline of culture," Wikipedia,
https://en.wikipedia.org/wiki/Outline_of_culture.

43. Dr. Christian Jarrett, "Different nationalities really have different personalities," *BBC Future,* April 13, 2017,
https://www.bbc.com/future/article/20170413-different-nationalities-really-have-different-personalities.

44. William F. Hutter, "Understanding the Dynamics of the Multi Generational Workforce," *The Human Resources Exchange Network,* December 3, 2008, https://www.hrexchangenetwork.com/hr-talent-management/articles/understanding-the-dynamics-of-the-multi-generation.

45. Ned Herrmann, "Whole Brain® Thinking is your Greatest Asset," Susie Leonard Weller (blog), https://www.susieweller.com/brain.html.

46. Ross Henley and Julie Jordan, "Neurodiversity," *Local Government Association,* https://www.local.gov.uk/lga-libdem-group/our-press-releases/neurodiversity.

47. C.E. Garcia, *Journal of Diversity in Higher Education,* 12(2), 181-193, https://psycnet.apa.org/doiLanding?doi=10.1037%2Fdhe0000126.

48. Jonathan Haidt, *The Righteous Mind: Why Good People Are Divided By Politics and Religion* (New York: Vintage Books, 2012), p. 64.

49. "Peanut Butter and Jelly Racism", New York Times, https://www.nytimes.com/video/us/100000004818663/peanut-butter-jelly-and-racism.html.

50. Pamela Fuller and Mark Murphy, *The Leader's Guide to Unconscious Bias: How To Reframe Bias, Cultivate Connection, and Create High-Performing Teams* (New York: Simon & Schuster 2020).

51. Erin Winkler, PhD, "When Do Kids Understand Race?," goop (blog), https://goop.com/wellness/parenthood/when-do-kids-understand-race/.

52. Adams, M., Bell, L. A., Griffin, P. (1997) *Teaching for Diversity and Social Justice,* (New York: Routledge 2016).

53. "The bias barrier: Allyships, inclusion, and everyday behaviors", *Deloitte,* https://www2.deloitte.com/content/dam/Deloitte/us/Documents/about-deloitte/inclusion-survey-research-the-bias-barrier.pdf.

54. "List of cognitive biases", *Wikipeadia,* https://en.wikipedia.org/wiki/List_of_cognitive_biases.

55. Jonathan Haidt, *The Righteous Mind: Why Good People Are Divided By Politics and Religion* (New York: Vintage Books, 2012), p.58.

56. Angeles Arrien, ed.,*Working Together* (San Francisco: Berrett-Koehler 2002), p. 149.

57. Jack Danielian, Patricia Gianotti, *Listening With Purpose: Entry Points To Shame And Narcissistic Vulnerability* (Plymouth, UK: Jason Aronson 2012).

58. A. Rob Hirschfeld, *Without Shame or Fear: From Adam to Christ* (New York: Church Publishing 2017), p. 30.

59. Thandika, *Learning to Be White: Money, Race, and God in America* (New York: Continuum Publishing Group 2002), p. 20.

60. Thandika, *Learning to Be White: Money, Race, and God in America* (New York: Continuum Publishing Group 2002), pg. 42 - 56.

61. Dr Michael Muthukrishna and Robbin Schimmelpfennig, "Resolving-the-paradox-of-diversity-How-can-we-reap-the-benefits-of-diversity-without-paying-the-costs-of-co-ordination ," *London School of Economics and Political Science*, December 13, 2021, https://www.lse.ac.uk/News/Latest-news-from-LSE/2021/l-december-21/Resolving-the-paradox-of-diversity-How-can-we-reap-the-benefits-of-diversity-without-paying-the-costs-of-co-ordination.

62. Michael I. Norton and Samuel R. Sommers, "Whites See Racism as a Zero-Sum Game That They Are Now Losing," *Harvard Business Review,* https://www.hbs.edu/ris/Publication%20Files/norton%20sommers%20whites%20see%20racism_ca92b4be-cab9-491d-8a87-cf1c6ff244ad.pdf).

63. Derald Wing Sue 1, Christina M Capodilupo, Gina C Torino, Jennifer M Bucceri, Aisha M B Holder, Kevin L Nadal, and Marta Esquilin, "Racial Micro-Aggressions in Everyday Life: Implications for Clinical Practice," *American Psychologist,* May-Jun 2007, https://pubmed.ncbi.nlm.nih.gov/17516773/.

64. Michael Morris, "Standard White: Dismantling White Normativity", California Law Review Vol. 104, No. 4 (August 2016), https://www.jstor.org/stable/24758741, pp. 949-978.

65. Peggy McIntosh, "White Privilege" video: https://www.youtube.com/watch?v=ysj_8fqnNcY; "White Privilege: Unpacking the Invisible Knapsack," https://psychology.umbc.edu/files/2016/10/White-Privilege_McIntosh-1989.pdf.

66. Keith Lawrence & Terry Keleher, "Chronic Disparity: Strong and Pervasive Evidence of Racial Inequalities - *Poverty Outcomes*: Structural Racism,"

(PDF), 2004, https://www.intergroupresources.com/rc/Definitions%20of%20Racism.pdf.

67. David A. Thomas and Robin J. Ely, "Making Differences Matter: A New Paradigm for Managing Diversity," *Harvard Business Review,* https://hbr.org/1996/09/making-differences-matter-a-new-paradigm-for-managing-diversity.

68. "The Age Diversity in the Workplace: How does it impact results?", *HR Magazine,* https://www.hrcloud.com/blog/the-age-diversity-in-the-workplace-how-does-it-impact-results.

69. "The Age Diversity in the Workplace: How does it impact results?" *HR Magazine,* August 13, 2021, https://www.hrcloud.com/blog/the-age-diversity-in-the-workplace-how-does-it-impact-results.

70. Ibid.

71. Curt J. Howes, Howes, <u>Organizational Performance: They Key to Success in the 21st Century</u> (Las Vegas: Xlibris 2021), P. 82.

72. Michael Lally, "20 of the Biggest Marketing Fails of All Time (and Why They Sucked)," Business 2 Community (blog), https://www.business2community.com/marketing/20-of-the-biggest-marketing-fails-of-all-time-and-why-they-sucked-02287809.

73. Jamie Page Deaton, "Why the Ford Edsel Failed," *how stuffworks,* https://auto.howstuffworks.com/why-the-ford-edsel-failed.htm#:~:text=Ugly%2C%20overpriced%2C%20overhyped%2C%20poorly,the%20case%20of%20the%20Edsel.

74. Greg Bailey, "4 Famous Project Management Failures and What to Learn from Them," *TempusResource,* October 8, 2018, https://www.prosymmetry.com/resources/4-famous-project-management-failures-and-what-to-learn-from-them/.

75. Curt J. Howes, Howes, <u>Organizational Performance: They Key to Success in the 21st Century</u> (Las Vegas: Xlibris 2021), p. 142.

76. <u>Ibid,</u> p. 178.

77. <u>Ibid,</u> p. 235.

78. <u>Ibid,</u> p. 251.

79. John P. Kotter, "Leading Change: Why Transformation Effort Fail," *Harvard Business Review*, May-June 1995, https://hbr.org/1995/05/leading-change-why-transformation-efforts-fail-2.

80. Kendra Cherry, "Learning Style Inventory Types and Their Uses", *verrywelmind*, November 23, 2020, https://www.verywellmind.com/what-is-a-learning-style-inventory-2795159.

81. Colleen Walsh, "Supreme Court to hear Harvard admissions challenge", *The Harvard Gazette*, January 24, 2022, https://news.harvard.edu/gazette/story/2022/01/supreme-court-to-take-harvard-admissions-case/.

82. Anastasia Reesa Tomkin, "The Case for Selective Discrimination", *NPQ*, November 18,2021, https://nonprofitquarterly.org/the-case-for-selective-discrimination/?mc_cid=b534415909&mc_eid=9ca06be6ba.

83. "The PwC Diversity Journey", *PwC*, September 2016, https://www.pwc.com/gx/en/diversity-inclusion/best-practices/assets/the-pwc-diversity-journey.pdf.

84. Angela Peacock, "Why Workplace Diversity Continues to Stagnate Without Accountability and Measurement," *affirmity* (blog), September 14, 2021, https://www.affirmity.com/blog/workplace-diversity-stagnates-without-accountability/.

85. "What Are Management Styles", *HRZONE*, https://www.hrzone.com/hr-glossary/what-are-management-styles.

86. Erika Johnson, "Top 4 Reasons Diversity and Inclusion Programs Fail," *Forbes*, March 29, 2021, https://www.forbes.com/sites/forbeseq/2021/03/29/top-4-reasons-diversity-and-inclusion-programs-fail/?sh=61f52bb77c84.

87. Kumar Parakala, "How To Overcome Barriers To Inclusion And Diversity," *Forbes*, June 17, 2021, https://www.forbes.com/sites/forbestechcouncil/2021/06/17/how-to-overcome-barriers-to-inclusion-and-diversity/?sh=72f4b78d6075.

88. M.T. Wroblewski "Negative Effects of Diversity in the Workplace," *Smallbusiness Chron*," March 4, 2019, https://smallbusiness.chron.com/difference-between-inter--intra-group-conflict-2658.html.

89., John Karren and Carolyn Lee, "Where are you on the D&I maturity curve?," *Price Waterhouse*, December 17, 2018, https://www.pwc.com/us/en/industries/industrial-products/industrial-insights/diversity-inclusion-maturity-curve.html.

90. Ibid.

91. Dara Barlin, <u>A New Kind of Power: Using Human-Centered leadership to drive innovation, equity, And Belonging In Government Institutions</u> (Amazon: EpicAuthor 2021), p. 25.

92. "7 Management Styles for Effective Leadership (With Examples)", *Indeed*, November 4, 2021, https://www.indeed.com/career-advice/career-development/management-styles?aceid=&gclid=Cj0KCQiA3rKQBhCNARIsACUEW_ZMO6MYZks7CydqVLWs_QChmny01S67YMe1Dpw1V2L8sgpnIIWSMV0aAiOeEALw_wcB.

93. "Health Equity Transformation Assessment: The Six Levers of Transformation," <u>AFA Institute for Diversity and Health Equity,</u> https://equity.aha.org/.

94. Curt J. Howes, Howes, <u>Organizational Performance: They Key to Success in the 21st Century</u> (Las Vegas: Xlibris 2021), p. 209.

95. "10 Types of Power in Leadership," *Indeed*, May 26, 2021https://www.indeed.com/career-advice/career-development/types-of-power-in-leadership.

96. "Pressing Toward Racial Equity," *District Management Journal, v.29, Spring 2021,* https://www.dmgroupk12.com/writable/documents/DMJ_29_Interview_FINAL.pdf pg. 9.

97. Madhuri Gupta, "PDCA – Dr Deming's Gift To The World", *The Art Of Positive Change* (blog), http://www.siobhaindanaher.com/pdca-dr-demings-gift-to-the-world/.

98. John P. Kotter, "Leading change: Why restoration efforts fail," *Harvard Business Review*, March/April 1995, https://hbr.org/1995/05/leading-change-why-transformation-efforts-fail-2.

99. "Difference between Values and Principles," *Difference.guru*, May 28, 2019, https://difference.guru/difference-between-values-and-principles/.

100. Frederic Laloux, "The future of management is real", *strategy+business*, Julyu 6, 2015, https://www.strategy-business.com/article/00344.

101. Smith, L. W. (2000). Stakeholder analysis: a pivotal practice of successful projects. Paper presented at Project Management Institute Annual Seminars & Symposium, Houston, TX. Newtown Square, PA: Project Management

Institute, https://www.pmi.org/learning/library/stakeholder-analysis-pivotal-practice-projects-8905.

102. Jayne Thompson, "Examples of Affirmative Action in a Workplace," *CHRON*, May 28, 2019 https://smallbusiness.chron.com/examples-affirmative-action-workplace-12019.html.

103. "Why Diversity Programs Fail: And what works better," *Harvard Business Review*, https://hbr.org/2016/07/why-diversity-programs-fail.

104. Vivian Hunt, Sara Prince, Sundiatu Dixon-Fyle, and Lareina Yee, "Delivering through Diversity", McKinsey & Company's 2018, https://www.mckinsey.com/~/media/McKinsey/Business%20Functions/Organization/Our%20Insights/Delivering%20through%20diversity/Delivering-through-diversity_full-report.ashx.

105. Balter, Roscoe; Chow, Joy; Jin, and Yin "What Diversity Metrics are Best Used to Track and Improve Employee Diversity?", *Cornell University Library*, March 7, 2014, https://ecommons.cornell.edu/handle/1813/74536.

106. Rebekah Steele, "Metrics that Matter: More than Diversity ROI", *The Conference Board*, Mach 7, 2016, https://www.conference-board.org/blog/postdetail.cfm?post=5117.

107. ISO 26,000 Guidance on Social Responsibility, *ISO*, https://www.iso.org/standard/42546.html.

108. G.T. Doran, "There's a S.M.A.R.T. way to write management's goals and objectives," *Management Rev*iew, 70 (11), 1981, 35–36 https://community.mis.temple.edu/mis0855002fall2015/files/2015/10/S.M.A.R.T-Way-Management-Review.pdf.

109. Jim Kirkpatrick and Wendy Kirkpatrick, "Stumped on How to Measure DEI Training," *td magazine*, October 2021, pg. 28-29.

110. Section 508 of the rehabilitation act of 1973, https://www.section508.gov/manage/laws-and-policies/.

111. Curt J. Howes, Howes, Organizational Performance: They Key to Success in the 21st Century (Las Vegas: Xlibris 2021), pg. 83.

112. "What Are the Top Ten Core Business Processes?," *Bizmanualz*, https://www.bizmanualz.com/improve-business-processes/what-are-the-top-ten-core-business-processes.html.

113. Michael E. Porter, "The Five Competitive Forces That Shape Strategy," *Harvard Business Review*, January 2008, https://hbr.org/2008/01/the-five-competitive-forces-that-shape-strategy.

114. "ISO 26,000 Guidance On Social Responsibility," https://www.iso.org/iso-26000-social-responsibility.html.

115. Curt J. Howes, Howes, Organizational Performance: They Key to Success in the 21st Century (Las Vegas: Xlibris 2021), p. 190-191.

116. Curt J. Howes, Howes, Organizational Performance: They Key to Success in the 21st Century (Las Vegas: Xlibris 2021), p. 278.

117. "Diversity Scorecards: Definition, Importance and How To Create One", *Indeed*, September 9, 2021 https://www.indeed.com/career-advice/career-development/what-is-diversity-scorecard.

118. "The 2021 CEO Blueprint for Racial Equity: What companies can do to advance racial equity and combat systemic racism in the workplace, communities, and society," Policylink, FSF, and Just Capital, June 2021, .https://corporateracialequityalliance.org/sites/default/files/2021%20CEO%20Blueprint%20for%20Racical%20Equity%20070121.pdf, pg. 9.

119. Jennifer Brown, How To Be An Inclusive Leader (Oakland: Berrett-Koehler Publishing 2019), pp. 19,43-46

120. Desiree Williams-Rajee, "Equity, Diversity and Inclusion in Recruitment, Hiring and Retention," (PDF) *Urban Sustainability Directors Network*, pg. 9, https://www.usdn.org/uploads/cms/documents/usdn-equity-in-recruitment_hiring_retention-100418update.pdf.

121. Angela Peacock, "Why Workplace Diversity Continues to Stagnate Without Accountability and Measurement," *affirmity* (blog), https://www.pdtglobal.com/workplace-diversity-stagnates-without-accountability/.

122. "Equitable Decision-Making Tool", Clark College, https://www.clark.edu/about/governance/shared-governance/EquitableDecisionMakingTool.pdf.

123. The Thinking Shop, https://thethinkingshop.org/.

124. Melanie Wolkoff Wachsman, "10 ways Companies can attract a diverse pool of job candidates," *TechRepublic*, August 28, 2020, https://www.techrepublic.com/article/10-ways-companies-can-attract-a-

diverse-pool-of-job-candidates/?ftag=TRE684d531&bhid=
28204757424522027431861037633352&mid=13013855&cid=2079628807.

125. Melanie Wolkoff Wachsman, "10 ways Companies can attract a diverse pool of job candidates," *TechRepublic*, August 28, 2020, https://www.techrepublic.com/article/10-ways-companies-can-attract-a-diverse-pool-of-job-candidates/?ftag=TRE684d531&bhid=
28204757424522027431861037633352&mid=13013855&cid=2079628807.

126. "10 Ways to Remove Gender Bias from Job Descriptions*", glassdoor for Employers* (blog), April 2021, https://www.glassdoor.com/employers/blog/10-ways-remove-gender-bias-job-listings/#:~:text=1)%20Use%20gender%20neutral%20titles%20in%20job%20descriptions&text=Avoid%20including%20words%20in%20your,%2C%22%20or%20%22developer.%22.

127. Derrick Thompson, "Besides Money, Recruit With Training," *TD magazine*, December 2021, p. 12.

128. Roy Maurer, "Employers Are Responding to Job Candidates Changing Expectations," *SHRM*, January 22, 2022, https://www.shrm.org/hr-today/news/all-things-work/Pages/employers-respond-to-job-candidates-changing-expectations.aspx.

129. Lin Grensing-Pophal, "Recruiting Retirees: Opportunities, Barriers and Best Practices," *SHRM*, December 14, 2021, https://www.shrm.org/resourcesandtools/hr-topics/talent-acquisition/pages/recruiting-retirees-opportunities-barriers-best-practices.aspx.

130. "How to Target Passive Job Seekers," *SHRM*, https://www.shrm.org/ResourcesAndTools/tools-and-samples/how-to-guides/Pages/How-to-Target-Passive-Job-Seekers.aspx.

131. "4 Areas You May Not Have Considered When Mitigating Hiring Bias," affirmity (blog), October 14, 2021, https://www.affirmity.com/blog/4-areas-you-may-not-have-considered-when-mitigating-hiring-bias.

132. Shilpa Pherwani and Cedar Pruitt, "What IS Equity?," Interactive Business Inclusion Solutions, https://www.ibisconsultinggroup.com/insight/what-is-equity/.

133. Talya N. Bauer, Ph.D, "Onboarding New Employees: Maximizing Success", *SHRM Foundation's Effective Practice Guidelines Series*.

134. "Equity, Diversity and Inclusion in Recruitment, Hiring and Retention", Urban Sustainability Directors Network,

https://www.usdn.org/uploads/cms/documents/usdn-equity-in-recruitment_hiring_retention-100418update.pdf, p.9.

135. Derrick Thompson, "Promote The Allyship and Amplification In The Workplace," *TD magazine*, December 2021, p.14.

136. Shilpa Pherwani and Cedar Pruitt, "What IS Equity?," Interactive Business Inclusion Solutions, https://www.ibisconsultinggroup.com/insight/what-is-equity/.

137. Shilpa Pherwani and Cedar Pruitt, "What IS Equity?," Interactive Business Inclusion Solutions, https://www.ibisconsultinggroup.com/insight/what-is-equity/.

138. Derrick Thompson, "Gens Y And Z Desire Respect Over Perks," *TD magazine*, October 2021, p. 12.

139. Mindtools, https://www.mindtools.com/pages/article/avoiding-psychological-bias.htm.

140. Fidelity DEI Plan, *Fidelity Investments*, https://www.fidelity.com/about-fidelity/citizenship#diversityandinclusion.

141. "BMC Medical Ethics" *BMC*, https://bmcmedethics.biomedcentral.com/.

142. Brian Good, "Airbnb Tests New 'Anonymous' Booking Process to Fight Potential Renter Racism," *DiversityInc*, January 5, 2022, https://www.diversityinc.com/airbnb-tests-new-anonymous-booking-process-to-fight-potential-renter-racism.

143. Stephanie Spellers, Erc H.F. Law, Companions on the Episcopal Way (New York: Church Publishing 2018), p. 83.

144. Doug Stone, Sheila Heen, and Bruce Patten, Difficult Conversations (New York: Penguin Books 1999), pg. 85.

Acknowledgements

In writing this book I have found out why everyone does not do so. It is a long and arduous task with many moving parts. The thinking necessary to write it draws from everything you have learned in life. It is a project involving a wide range of disciplines. So, my deepest thanks go to the many individuals who helped manifest me and this book. Without you, this book would not exist.

Special Thanks go the following wonderful people.

To my parents, James Sr. and Mary who pushed me to think beyond the regular and the usual. To always see opportunity in everyone and everything. They set me up for success.

To my wife Nancy who spent many days and evenings listening to me on the phone interviewing people and doing research for this book.

To the Rev. Bill Exner and Bishop Gene Robinson who recognized in me the ability to help address the divisions that exist in our society and created opportunities for me to recognize my call to address them.

To Caroline Fairless for being so open about her own journey in writing and living. She helped me put how society operates into perspective and think through what this book could and should be.

To Curt J. Howes whose book <u>Organizational Performance: The Key to Success in the 21st Century,</u> I quote frequently in this book. Curt provided a perfect framework for me to express my thoughts about DEI. I am so grateful for the time he took to meet with me and the wisdom he imparted.

To the many people with whom I spoke gathering data, especially Aura Huot, Armando Llorente, Nannan Hu, Nick Holmes, Dara Barlin, Barbara Boldt, Guy Powell, Julie Delucca Collins, Kelly Waltman, Rose Kattackal, Matt Mowry, Ernesto Burden, Julie Alig, Sharon Mertz, Talmira Hill, Constance Cherise, and Grace Mattern for your insights that helped shape the book.

To my publisher, Trevor Crane, and the entire Epic Author Publishing team. I am so grateful to have found you. Your energy and enthusiasm uplifted me at times when I really needed it. Thank You for being who you are and truly desiring success for me (and others going through the process) in business and life.

Thanks to my editor, Ruth Mills, for enforcing the discipline of a book writer for this first-time out book author.

For reading this book, you are entitled to:

One free seat in an upcoming DEI workshop
(see workshops at www.organizationalignition.com)

OR

30 minutes of time with me

OR

A copy of my DEI Roadmap

To redeem your bonus, contact me at
James.Mckim@organizationalignition.com
with the subject "Book Bonus".

About the Author

James T. McKim is Founder and Managing Partner of Organizational Ignition, a management consulting firm. He is a sought-after consultant, facilitator, speaker, and author of the bestselling book The Diversity Factor: Igniting Superior Organizational Performance. Over his 35+ year career, he has helped small and large organizations, for-profit and non-profit, spark efficiency and growth through the aligning of people, process, and technology.

Mr. McKim is known nationally for his current focus on organizational and individual performance through diversity, equity, and inclusion (DEI). He is recognized by industry watchers such as Atd, Brandon Hall, Bersin Associates, Axelos, and PMI for his dedication to creating win-win situations between organizations and their employees. In addition to founding two companies, he has held senior leadership roles at organizations such as Hewlett Packard Enterprise, Fidelity, Dartmouth Hitchcock, and the Massachusetts Partnership for Diversity in Education in defining and executing strategic plans with an eye toward organizational performance.

Believing strongly in giving back to the community, Mr. McKim has facilitated startup and growth of statewide organizations such as the Economic Vitality New Hampshire and the Software Association of New Hampshire. He has played an active role in the shaping of public policy affecting the Technology industry. He serves, currently on several Boards playing leading roles as Chair of the NH PBS Finance Committee, Chair of the Episcopal Church's National Executive Council Committee Anti-Racism, and President of the Manchester NAACP.

To connect with Mr. McKim regarding selected speaking engagements or advice on your organizational performance efforts visit www.organizationalignition.com or connect with him at:

James.McKim@OrganizationalIgnition.com or
www.linkedin.com/jtmckimjr

Printed in the USA
CPSIA information can be obtained
at www.ICGtesting.com
LVHW020600111123
763660LV00025B/137